~

a Book
of
vigils

~

a Book
of
vigils

Christopher L. Webber

✠ CHURCH

Church Publishing Incorporated, New York

Copyright © 2002 by Christopher L. Webber

Library of Congress Cataloging-in-Publication Data
A book of vigils / [edited by] Christopher L. Webber.
   p. cm.
   ISBN 0-89869-383-7 (pbk.)
      1. Vigils (Liturgy) I. Webber, Christopher.
BV185 .B66 2002
264'.7—dc21

                       2002031337

Church Publishing Incorporated
445 Fifth Avenue
New York NY 10016

www.churchpublishing.org

5 4 3 2 1

special thanks

Special thanks are due to the Rt. Rev. George Packard who initiated this project by asking me to produce materials for a vigil for peace and justice to be held by the Episcopal Peace Fellowship and others before his consecration as Bishop of the Armed Forces and Chaplaincies. I am grateful also to the Diocese of Connecticut for providing the opportunity to develop A Vigil before the Election or Consecration of a Bishop for the consecration of the Rt. Rev. James Curry and the Rt. Rev. Wilfrido Ramos-Orench.

table of contents

întroòuctíon
to a
Book of vígíls

What is a vigil?

The keeping of vigils in the form of extended periods of nighttime prayer is an ancient Christian tradition; there is evidence of vigils as early as the first years of the second century. Vigils probably began as a way for Christians to follow Jesus' repeated teaching about the importance of watchful waiting to the spiritual life; perhaps they were held at night because of a belief that the second coming would be at midnight. At first these vigils seem to have been kept only at Easter, but eventually vigils were kept also on the feasts of martyrs and, later, on certain major feast days—such as Pentecost—as well. In the Middle Ages, however, vigils became increasingly the province of monastic orders and were unfamiliar to other Christians except for those keeping the Easter Vigil in the Eastern Church. In modern times, the Easter Vigil gradually has regained its central place in the West, with Vatican II and various prayer book revisions—including the Episcopal Church's 1979 Book of Common Prayer—giving official sanction to the practice.

The keeping of vigils seems to satisfy a deeply felt need; modern revival of the idea of coming together for extended periods of prayer began as a popular, rather than an institutional, trend in the church and society. In addition to the strongly reestablished Easter Vigil, vigils after the evening service on Maundy Thursday also have become common occurrences. Even more striking are some of the newer applications of the ancient form of the vigil. The Christmas midnight service is largely a modern invention without precedent in the early church's life; although it is not truly a vigil, several aspects of the service, such as the nighttime setting and the watchful expectancy it conveys, draw from—and are inspired by—ancient vigil practice. Then there is the emerging practice of keeping vigils for special needs: for someone critically ill, or in times of national crisis, or before the election or consecration of a bishop (or the election of other

1

ministers). This topicality in the keeping of vigils may be the most innovative—and most valuable—expression of the modern vigil.

Vigils can have either a very public or a very private character. The early church's vigils were events for the whole community, while those of the Middle Ages were kept largely by members of monastic communities. In modern times, we are familiar on the one hand with the congregational keeping of Easter vigils and the gathering of larger communities for special public events, and on the other hand with the keeping of vigils by a few individuals through the night, often signing up for an hour or two by turns. Such "private" vigils offer the individual an opportunity to spend time in the silence through which God often speaks most directly; they provide a way for those keeping the vigil to offer themselves to God on behalf of others, to become more effective means of grace; they provide the opening into human life through which grace may flow into the world.

Regardless of the size of the vigil and the nature of the occasion—whether it is a single person meditating at a candlelit altar in the middle of the night on Maundy Thursday or a throng of people crowded into a huge cathedral trying to help one another make sense of a recent local or national tragedy—all vigils have one thing in common: they somehow manage to be both very intense and very peaceful. The spirit of a vigil is well described in a novel by Ellis Peters in which a Brother Cadfael (subsequently the hero of a television series) spends the night in prayer before removing a saint's relics to a new shrine:

> Brother Columbanus bowed humbly low to the altar, and took his place at the desk on the right. Brother Cadfael settled solidly at the one on the left, and with practised movements sought and found the best place for his knees. Stillness came down on them gently. He composed himself for a long watch.... Great darkness and constant, feeble light, the slow flowing of time from far beyond his conception and too far beyond his power to follow, the solitude about him and the troubled and peopled world within, all these settled into their perpetual pattern, a steady rhythm as perfect as sleep. He thought no more of Columbanus, he forgot that Columbanus existed. He prayed as he breathed, forming no words and making no specific requests, only holding in his heart, like broken birds in cupped hands, all those people who were in stress or grief because of their little saint, for if he suffered like this for their sake, how much more must she feel for them?

> —*Ellis Peters,* A Morbid Taste for Bones, *Fawcett Crest, 1977, p. 160*

Using this book

The need for some vigils can arise suddenly, leaving those arranging them very little time to plan. The vigils provided in this book that fall into this topical category, such as vigils for the sick or in time of crisis, should be thought of as outlines or samples, not as liturgies to be followed verbatim. Some of the material provided here may be appropriate to the circumstances and to the people involved, but other material may not. Even the vigils provided here for events that will not come as a surprise (such as the recurring feasts of Maundy Thursday and Pentecost or the election of a bishop or other minister) may not have universal application for all worshipers in all places and times. The size of the group involved, the prevailing worship style of a given community, and many other variables may require substantial changes to the patterns supplied here.

Readings for each vigil are provided from the Bible and other sources, but more are provided than are likely to be needed for all but the longest vigils. All readings should be read slowly, as if the reader is discovering the words for the first time. The words, however, are not there simply to be instructional but to be a tool of meditation, as an opening point for God to guide the thoughts of each person wherever God will. Those who listen to the prayers and readings of a vigil should let the rhythms of the body, such as thinking and breathing, slow down from the usual pace. This is God's time, not a commodity to be consumed and discarded. Use it well. Let God use it not only for the sake of the participants but also for others.

But even more important than the words used in a vigil are the silences. Regardless of the readings used, it is always important to leave the larger part of the time for silent watching and waiting. An emphasis on silence may be more easily achieved during a vigil involving only one person, but even in a large, public vigil, silence should be an important ingredient. Participants should let God guide their words, their thoughts, and their silence. Above all, vigils are for listening and being open to the working of God's spirit within.

Each vigil is organized on a similar segmented plan, with each segment containing prayers, readings, psalms or hymns, and silence. Segments are designed to take about twenty minutes but might last thirty minutes to an hour, depending on the length of the silence. For some people, five minutes may be as much silence at one time as they can observe without becoming uncomfortable; others who are accustomed to silent meditation may prefer to spend twenty or thirty minutes or even more before moving on to another reading or formal prayer. In a public vigil, an address by a religious or civic leader might be added to each section and the time for silence reduced—but not eliminated!

Planning a vigil

The planning processes for large vigils, private vigils, occasional vigils, and recurring vigils are all very different. A large, public vigil in a national or local emergency will require a committee of local leaders, because of the complicated demands for any such event, all of which will need to be dealt with rapidly. The need for a vigil in time of sickness or death also may arise suddenly but, unlike any large, public vigil, usually can be organized by a few concerned individuals in a short time. Those planning a vigil before the election or consecration of a bishop rarely have to do their planning on short notice (usually there are months of planning time available), but the scope of such an event can be enormous if the entire diocese is to be sufficiently informed and involved. Vigils kept during the recurring major feasts of the church year have still another set of challenges; if such a vigil is being introduced into a community's worship for the first time, considerable education of the worshipers may be required beforehand, but if the vigil is a long-standing tradition in the community, only minor annual revisions to the liturgy may be required. Some suggestions for each of these three situations follow.

A national or local emergency

For a large, public vigil in a time of national or local emergency, the materials provided for A Vigil in the Presence of God and A Vigil for Peace and Justice may be the most appropriate. The simplest plan for such a vigil involves segments of fifteen to thirty minutes, each including a reading, psalm, and prayer as well as time for silence. As stated earlier, location, timing, leadership, and so on will vary greatly depending on the circumstances.

Times of sickness or death

Vigils in times of sickness or death will vary depending upon the exact circumstances and upon the people most directly involved. Such a vigil may be set up on the spur of the moment by a handful of people at the bedside of a sick or dying friend. With a bit of planning, a larger group may be involved, either watching and praying together for an hour or two as a group or individually, one after the other, for several hours, even through the night. Decisions to be made include the following:

Location: A local church or chapel may be convenient, especially when someone has died. In time of sickness, a vigil may be kept in a church or chapel, a hospital room (or hospital chapel), or even a private home.

Duration: A vigil in time of sickness may be kept for many hours or at a set time every day for a period of time. In time of death, a vigil may be kept for an hour or several hours in the evening before the funeral or even through the night until the time of the service.

Leadership: A vigil may be kept by a group with a leader or leaders to read the lessons and lead the psalms, or it may be kept in turns by one or two people at a time, reading and praying silently by using a printed vigil guide.

Materials: Determine whether all the vigil readings, prayers, psalms, and instructions will be gathered in one printed document or whether only an outline—with Prayer Book and Bible references—will be provided.

The election or consecration of a bishop

Decisions to be made include the following:

Location: A vigil might be kept in the cathedral, or vigil materials may be compiled, printed, and distributed to several centers around the diocese, or to any parish that wishes to participate. If there are several locations, the vigils might occur prior to the election or consecration at a time convenient to each separate community, or the timing for all the vigils might be synchronous; if there are several locations and each is for a large, public vigil, then each center or parish might agree to fill a specific one- or two-hour vigil time slot so as to create one long, uninterrupted "chain" of diocesan prayer vigils—an arrangement modeled on the sign-up-sheet approach to the traditional all-night Maundy Thursday vigil.

Duration: A vigil might be kept for an hour or two during the day, or in the evening, or from a set time until midnight, or until morning, or until the election process or consecration begins. Large, public vigils probably should last only an hour or two. Vigils during which one person or small groups take turns keeping watch may last for many hours, even through the night. An all-night vigil might begin with Evening Prayer; Compline might be inserted at the appropriate hour; Morning Prayer might conclude such a vigil.

Participation: Unless the vigil is being kept for an hour or two by a large number, a sign-up sheet might be provided for individuals who agree to keep the vigil for a set time of one or more hours, thereby ensuring that the vigil is fully maintained. Parishes of the diocese might be asked to provide these individuals, or the planning committee might call on a diocesan organization—such as a diocesan chapter of the Anglican Fellowship of Prayer, the Brotherhood of St. Andrew, or diocesan altar guild—to recruit support for the plan.

Printing: Notices, sign-up sheets, and guidelines for keeping the vigil will need to be printed well in advance. Materials for meditation during the vigil need to be provided; these materials may be compiled and printed out in full or else supplied as easy-to-follow outlines which refer the user to the appropriate pages in the Prayer Book, Bible, or other books.

Adaptation: For simplicity's sake, the vigil model supplied here is for the election or consecration of a bishop, but it can easily be adapted to the appointment of a deacon, priest or any other church leader or minister (see notes for A Vigil before the Election or Consecration of a Bishop).

Safety concerns

The safety and security issues to be considered whenever a vigil is kept through the night in a church or chapel deserve special mention here. There should always be at least two individuals present, and they should have a cell phone handy or know where the nearest phone is. Since many vigils are kept by candlelight, have a fire extinguisher handy—just in case. Safety issues will vary from vigil site to vigil site and should be given serious consideration during the planning process.

~

a vigil
in the
presence
of god

~

NOTES FOR

a vigil in the presence of god

The material provided here for prayer and meditation centers attention on the presence of God: recalling God's presence, being open to God's presence, being present to God. It can be used with any of the other vigils in this book (except the vigil for the Eve of Pentecost) or separately. Begin the time with prayer, using one or more of the passages provided. Use the words provided here as a framework for your prayer, then let your own life and the guidance of the Spirit enlarge upon that framework. Spend most of your time in silence: waiting, listening, using the Jesus Prayer or any other centering devices you find useful.

The Jesus Prayer is an ancient method of prayer that comes to us from the Russian Orthodox tradition. It consists of repeating the sentence, "Lord Jesus Christ, Son of the Living God, have mercy on me a sinner," or, more simply, "Lord Jesus Christ, have mercy on me." This is said slowly and meditatively, preferably in time with one's breathing, so that the address ("Lord Jesus, etc.") is said as breath is drawn in, and the petition ("have mercy, etc.") is said as one breathes out.

The vigil model presented here provides an opening prayer followed by four segments, each one of which contains a reading, a psalm or hymn, and a prayer. The model is intended for a private vigil but can also be used for a large public vigil with readers for the readings and a leader who directs the liturgy and leads the prayers, hymns, and psalms.

For a private vigil

For a private vigil, simply have these materials or materials modeled on them ready for those keeping the vigil. If the vigil is to be kept for many hours, it is usually best to ask individuals to volunteer for one or more hours and to assign two segments for each hour. Those keeping the vigil would begin with the opening prayer, spend a half hour on each of the two segments assigned, and conclude with the closing prayers. There should be no uncertainty among participants about which segments they have been assigned.

For long, private vigils, you may wish to provide a liturgical way for each participant to mark his or her cumulative contribution to the ongoing prayer. One way to do this is with candles: each participant lights a candle before beginning and leaves it burning to be joined by other candles as the turns come and go. The last participant concludes the vigil on behalf of the group by extinguishing the candles. The practice of burning candles throughout much of the night, however, presents serious safety concerns. Very tall votive candles may prove safer than tapers which can fall from their holders. Never leave burning candles unattended. If candles are to be used, at least two individuals should be in the vigil space at all times.

For a public vigil

If this material is used as part of a public vigil, hymns and talks by civic and religious leaders also may be added. The recommended order is as follows: 1) reading; 2) psalm or hymn (the hymns printed here after the readings are intended to be read like psalms); 3) prayer; 4) talk by civic or religious leader; 5) hymn to be sung by the congregation. Additional instructions for public prayer are as follows:

Prayers: Beginning with the opening prayer ("You are great, O God, and worthy of highest praise") and for every prayer thereafter, the leader says, "Let us pray" (if the leader is to pray aloud on behalf of the assembly) or "Let us pray the following prayer together" (if the assembly is to join in).

Psalms: Before each psalm, the leader says, "Let us say Psalm [number] responsively"; or, "Let us say Psalm [number] together." For hymns that follow the readings, the leader says, "Let us say the words of the hymn together." For responsive readings for large ecumenical gatherings, print the congregation's responses in italics.

Readings: The reader announces each reading as indicated. After the reading, the reader remains in place, keeping the silence. If there is some concern that less experienced readers may rush the silence, have an unobtrusive watch or small clock at the podium so that the silence is kept for an appropriate length of time. The silence concludes when the reader proclaims the brief, epigraphic "echo" from the previous reading; these epigraphs appear in the vigil text immediately following the rubric "Silence."

Segments: The text is divided into four segments, each prefaced with a "title" that states a theme as follows: I. The Importance of Prayer; II. How is God's Presence Known?; III. The Vision of God; IV. The Vision of God in Christ. If the liturgy you are planning will be multimedia, you may wish to use an overhead projector to flash these titles before the assembly at the appropriate moment. In addition, or instead, the leader may establish the theme of each segment by saying the following:

> *Segment I:* The next part of our vigil will help us focus our thoughts on the importance of prayer.

> *Segment II:* The next part of our vigil will help us turn our thoughts to the ways in which God's presence is known.

Segment III: In the next part of our vigil, we reflect on the vision of God.

Segment IV: In the final part of our vigil, we reflect on the vision of God in Christ.

Note that this vigil also may serve as the "First Hour" for the much longer Vigil for Peace and Justice (see notes for A Vigil for Peace and Justice below).

a vigil in the presence of god

OPENING PRAYER

You are great, O God, and worthy of highest praise:
you stir in us the joy of praising you,
since you have made us for yourself,
and our hearts are restless
until they find rest in you.

> *One thing have I asked of the LORD,*
> *one thing I seek:*
> *that I may dwell in the house of the LORD all the days*
> *of my life*
> *to behold the fair beauty of the LORD*
> *and to seek him in his temple.*
> *For God alone my soul in silence waits;*
> *from him comes my salvation.*
> *—Psalms 27:5–6; 62:1*

God of peace,
let us rest in your presence,
let us keep watch in your holy place,
let our restless thoughts be stilled,
let your peace sink deep into our souls,
let your presence be sufficient for us,
as we keep watch before you.

O Israel, wait for the Lord, for with the Lord there is mercy;
let that mercy be with those who keep watch this night;
with those who seek for peace in human hearts
in places of conflict and tension;
with those who preach the gospel
to those who have not heard it;

with those who witness to your love
>to those who have not seen it;
with those who work for healing tonight
>in places of conflict,
>in hospitals and homes;
with those who bring your presence
>to those who need your love and healing power.

Be present, Lord Christ, with those who watch this night;
with those who are ill;
with those who are dying;
with those who are hungry;
with those who are homeless;
with those who rejoice
>in the birth of a child,
>in a marriage,
>in an anniversary,
>in prayers answered,
>in the gift of love,
>in the confidence of faith;
with those who wait for the Spirit's gift;
and grant that our waiting and watching this night
>may draw us closer to your love,
and make us more faithful servants of your purpose. Amen.

I. THE IMPORTANCE OF PRAYER

A Reading from *Man's Quest for God* by Abraham Heschel

As a tree torn from the soil, as a river separated from its source, the human soul wanes when detached from what is greater than itself. Without the holy, the good turns chaotic; without the good, beauty becomes accidental. It is the pattern of the impeccable which makes the average possible. It is the attachment to what is spiritually superior: loyalty to a sacred person or idea, devotion to a noble friend or teacher, love for a people or for mankind, which holds our inner life together. But any ideal, human, social, or artistic, if it forms a roof over all of life, shuts us off from the light. Even the palm of one hand may bar the light of the entire sun. Indeed, we must be open to the remote in order to perceive the near. Unless we aspire to the utmost, we shrink to inferiority. Prayer is our attachment to the utmost. Without God in sight, we are like the scattered rungs of a broken ladder. To pray is to become a ladder on which thoughts mount to God to join the movement toward Him which surges unnoticed throughout the entire universe. We do not step out of the world when we pray; we merely see the world in a different setting. The self is not the hub, but the spoke of the revolving wheel. In prayer we shift the center of living from self-consciousness to self-surrender. God is the center toward which all forces tend. He is the source, and we are the flowing of His force, the ebb and flow of His tides.

—*Abraham Heschel*, Man's Quest for God,
Charles Scribner's Sons, 1954, pp. 6–7

Silence.

...God is the center...

Psalm 84 *Quam dilecta!*

1 How dear to me is your dwelling, O LORD of hosts! *
My soul has a desire and longing for the courts of the LORD;
my heart and my flesh rejoice in the living God.

2 The sparrow has found her a house
and the swallow a nest where she may lay her young; *
by the side of your altars, O LORD of hosts,
my King and my God.

3 Happy are they who dwell in your house! *
they will always be praising you.

4 Happy are the people whose strength is in you! *
whose hearts are set on the pilgrims' way.

5 Those who go through the desolate valley will find it a place of springs, *
for the early rains have covered it with pools of water.

6 They will climb from height to height, *
and the God of gods will reveal himself in Zion.

7 LORD God of hosts, hear my prayer; *
hearken, O God of Jacob.

8 Behold our defender, O God; *
and look upon the face of your Anointed.

9 For one day in your courts is better than
   a thousand in my own room, *
   and to stand at the threshold of the house of my God
   than to dwell in the tents of the wicked.

10 For the LORD God is both sun and shield; *
   he will give grace and glory;

11 No good thing will the LORD withhold *
   from those who walk with integrity.

12 O LORD of hosts, *
   happy are they who put their trust in you!

Prayer

Lord, my God, teach my heart where and how to seek you,
   where and how to find you.
Lord, if you are not here,
   where shall I look for you in your absence?
Yet if you are everywhere,
   why do I not see you when you are present?
But surely you dwell in "light inaccessible."
   And where is light inaccessible?
   How shall I approach light inaccessible?
Or who will lead me and bring me into it
   that I may see you there?
And then, by what signs and under what forms shall I seek you?
   I have never seen you, Lord my God;
   I do not know your face.

Look upon us, Lord,
hear us and enlighten us,
show us your true self.
Restore yourself to us that it may go well with us
   whose life is so evil without you.
Take pity on our efforts and our striving toward you,
for we have no strength apart from you.

Teach me to seek you,
>   and when I seek you show yourself to me,
>   for I cannot seek you unless you teach me;
>   nor can I find you unless you show yourself to me.

Let me seek you in desiring you
>   and desire you in seeking you,
>   find you in loving you
>   and love you in finding you. Amen.

—from the Proslogion of Anselm, Archbishop of Canterbury,
as quoted in Readings for the Daily Office from the Early Church,
J. Robert Wright, Church Publishing Incorporated, pp. 7–8.

II. HOW IS GOD'S PRESENCE KNOWN?

A Reading from the First Book of Kings

Then the word of the LORD came to him, saying, "What are you doing here, Elijah?" He answered, "I have been very zealous for the LORD, the God of hosts; for the Israelites have forsaken your covenant, thrown down your altars, and killed your prophets with the sword. I alone am left, and they are seeking my life, to take it away." He said, "Go out and stand on the mountain before the LORD, for the LORD is about to pass by." Now there was a great wind, so strong that it was splitting mountains and breaking rocks in pieces before the LORD, but the LORD was not in the wind; and after the wind an earthquake, but the LORD was not in the earthquake; and after the earthquake a fire, but the LORD was not in the fire; and after the fire a sound of sheer silence. When Elijah heard it, he wrapped his face in his mantle and went out and stood at the entrance of the cave. Then there came a voice to him that said, "What are you doing here, Elijah?"

—1 Kings 19:9–13

Silence.

...a sound of sheer silence...

Hymn

God himself is with us; let us all adore him,
and with awe appear before him.
God is here within us,
souls in silence fear him,
humbly, fervently draw near him.
Now his own who have known
God, in worship lowly,
yield their spirits wholly.

Thou pervadest all things; let thy radiant beauty
light mine eyes to see my duty.
As the tender flowers
eagerly unfold them,
to the sunlight calmly hold them,
so let me quietly
in thy rays imbue me;
let thy light shine through me.

Come, abide within me; let my soul, like Mary,
be thine earthly sanctuary.
Come, indwelling Spirit,
with transfigured splendor;
love and honor will I render.
Where I go here below,
let me bow before thee,
know thee, and adore thee.

—*Gerhardt Tersteegen (1697–1769)*
Hymn #475, stanzas 1,3,4, The Hymnal 1982,
Church Publishing Incorporated

Prayer

Let me not live apart from you,
    O Giver of Life,
    my breath, my life, my joy,
    and the salvation of the world.
Therefore I come to you
    seeking forgiveness
    and the gift of your presence in my life.
Therefore I fall before you
    and implore you to come to me
    as you came to Matthew in his work,
    as you came to Mary and Martha in their home,
    as you came to the disciples on the road to Emmaus.
Come to me, Lord, I pray,
    in my home, in my work, in my travel;
    purify my heart,
    guide my thoughts,
    and direct all that I do
    by your presence in my life. Amen.

III.   THE VISION OF GOD

A Reading from the Book of Revelation

After this I looked, and there in heaven a door stood open! And the first voice, which I had heard speaking to me like a trumpet, said, "Come up here, and I will show you what must take place after this." At once I was in the spirit, and there in heaven stood a throne, with one seated on the throne! And the one seated there looks like jasper and carnelian, and around the throne is a rainbow that looks like an emerald. Around the throne are twenty-four thrones, and seated on the thrones are twenty-four elders, dressed in white robes, with golden crowns on their heads. Coming from the throne are flashes of lightning, and rumblings and peals of thunder, and in front of the throne burn seven flaming torches, which are the seven spirits of God; and in front of the throne there is something like a sea of glass, like crystal. Around the throne, and on each side of the throne, are four living creatures, full of eyes in front and behind: the first living creature like a lion, the second living creature like an ox, the third living creature with a face like a human face, and the fourth living creature like a flying eagle. And the four living creatures, each of them with six wings, are full of eyes all around and inside. Day and night without ceasing they sing, "Holy, holy, holy, the Lord God the Almighty, who was and is and is to come."

—Revelation 4:1–8

Silence.

...Holy, holy, holy, the Lord God the Almighty...

Psalm 62:1–2, 8–9 *Nonne Deo?* &
Psalm 63:1–8 *Deus, Deus meus*

  62:1 For God alone my soul in silence waits; *
from him comes my salvation.

    2 He alone is my rock and my salvation, *
my stronghold, so that I shall not be greatly shaken.

    8 In God is my safety and my honor; *
God is my strong rock and my refuge.

    9 Put your trust in him always, O people, *
pour out your hearts before him, for God is our refuge.

63:1 O God, you are my God; eagerly I seek you; *
    my soul thirsts for you, my flesh faints for you,
    as in a barren and dry land where there is no water.

2 Therefore I have gazed upon you in your holy place, *
    that I might behold your power and your glory.

3 For your loving-kindness is better than life itself; *
    my lips shall give you praise.

4 So will I bless you as long as I live *
    and lift up my hands in your Name.

5 My soul is content, as with marrow and fatness, *
    and my mouth praises you with joyful lips,

6 When I remember you upon my bed, *
    and meditate on you in the night watches.

7 For you have been my helper, *
    and under the shadow of your wings I will rejoice.

8 My soul clings to you; *
    your right hand holds me fast.

Prayer

O God, who wonderfully created
    and yet more wonderfully renewed our human nature;
    grant us to be sharers of his divine nature
        who was willing to be a partaker of our humanity;
the same Jesus Christ our Lord,
    who lives and reigns with you
    in the unity of the Holy Spirit,
    God, world without end. Amen.

—*from the Leonine Sacramentary,*
as quoted in Holy Communion: An Anthology of Christian Devotion,
Massey Shepherd, Seabury Press, 1959, p. 30

IV. The Vision of God in Christ

A Reading from the Gospel according to St. Luke

Now about eight days after these sayings Jesus took with him Peter and John and James, and went up on the mountain to pray, and while he was praying, the appearance of his face changed, and his clothes became dazzling white. Suddenly they saw two men, Moses and Elijah, talking to him. They appeared in glory and were speaking of his departure, which he was about to accomplish at Jerusalem. Now Peter and his companions were weighed down with sleep; but since they had stayed awake, they saw his glory and the two men who stood with him. Just as they were leaving him, Peter said to Jesus, "Master, it is good for us to be here; let us make three dwellings, one for you, one for Moses, and one for Elijah"—not knowing what he said. While he was saying this, a cloud came and overshadowed them; and they were terrified as they entered the cloud. Then from the cloud came a voice that said, "This is my Son, my Chosen; listen to him!" When the voice had spoken, Jesus was found alone. And they kept silent and in those days told no one any of the things they had seen.

—Luke 9:28–36

Silence.

...listen to him...

Psalm 29 *Afferte Domino*

1 Ascribe to the LORD, you gods, *
    ascribe to the LORD glory and strength.

2 Ascribe to the LORD the glory due his Name; *
    worship the LORD in the beauty of holiness.

3 The voice of the LORD is upon the waters;
    the God of glory thunders; *
    the LORD is upon the mighty waters.

4 The voice of the LORD is a powerful voice; *
    the voice of the LORD is a voice of splendor.

5 The voice of the LORD breaks the cedar trees; *
    the LORD breaks the cedars of Lebanon;

6 He makes Lebanon skip like a calf, *
    and Mount Hermon like a young wild ox.

7 The voice of the LORD splits the flames of fire;
   the voice of the LORD shakes the wilderness; *
   the LORD shakes the wilderness of Kadesh.

8 The voice of the LORD makes the oak trees writhe *
   and strips the forests bare.

9 And in the temple of the LORD *
   all are crying, "Glory!"

10 The LORD sits enthroned above the flood; *
    the LORD sits enthroned as King for evermore.

11 The LORD shall give strength to his people; *
    the LORD shall give his people the blessing of peace.

Prayer

You, O Lord, are always present
   in this world,
   in those I meet,
   in human need,
   and in my heart,
but I am often blind and deaf to you.

Open my eyes, my Creator, Redeemer, and Sanctifier,
   to know you in the world you have made,
   to see you in the lives of others,
   to listen to you
         in the promptings of my heart and mind
   so that I may know you, see you, hear you,
         and make you known
   and give you glory in all things.

O God of peace, you have taught us that, in returning and rest, we shall be saved, in quietness and in confidence shall be our strength; now lift us, we pray, by the power of your Holy Spirit to your presence, where we may be still, and know that you are God. Amen.

—*The Book of Common Prayer, p. 832, alt.*

20

~

a vigil
for peace
and
justice

~

NOTES FOR
a vigil for peace and justice

The keeping of a Vigil for Peace and Justice is appropriate for, and spiritually beneficial to, a large, public gathering or individuals taking turns in keeping vigils that last for several hours. The material as provided here is more appropriate to a long, private vigil, and some adaptation will be required for public gatherings.

For private vigils

The material is presented in four very long sections called "hours." The model for the First Hour ("The Presence of God") has not been printed here; if you wish to follow a four-hour model, use the previous vigil in this book, A Vigil in the Presence of God, as the model for the first hour. The Second Hour ("The Peace of God"), the Third Hour ("The Justice of God"), and the Fourth Hour ("The Mercy of God") may be used as is or followed closely as models. Each hour is divided into four "segments" which are similar in length and content to the roman numeral vigil segments used elsewhere in this book. In addition, there is a section called "Closing Prayers" at the very end of the vigil.

There are readings, psalms (or hymns), prayers, and silences in each of the four segments for each hour. If these silences are kept as intended, and if the keepers of the vigil meditate upon each reading, psalm, hymn, or prayer, then each so-called vigil "hour" should indeed last an hour or even longer. Each individual (or small group) may keep one vigil hour, with the first participant(s) taking the First Hour, the second taking the Second Hour, and so on. Make sure each participant knows which hour she/he is to keep. If the vigil is to last longer than four hours, begin the cycle again. Note that each hour has its own concluding prayer, but the "Closing Prayers" section at the very end of the vigil (following the Fourth Hour) may, if desired, be used to conclude each and every participants' hour of vigil; in this way, vigils are kept differently in some ways and, in others, are kept in common.

Once you have determined the length of your vigil and the number of participants, and have assembled all the rubrics, prayers, psalms, and hymns, make a sufficient number of copies: 1) one for each person signed up to keep the vigil or; 2) two or three "master copies," which will remain in place as people come and go, keeping their hours of watch. Provide any other useful meditation materials, such as separate "bulletin insert" copies of the Jesus Prayer, which is a centering device suggested throughout this vigil. You also may wish to provide insert copies of the "Closing Prayers" section, if that section is to be used by every participant.

You may wish to use candles—one lighted by each participant—as a way to mark the cumulative prayers as the vigil progresses. See notes for a Vigil in the Presence of God for more information on the Jesus prayer and the use of candles.

For public vigils

There are more readings, prayers, hymns, and psalms provided in these four "hours" of material than can be fitted into a large, public occasion. Remember also that it may be appropriate to include speakers in a vigil devoted to justice and peace. Do not include so much material that the pace will be rushed in order to get through it all in a reasonable amount of time. Always allow ample time for silences.

Those planning the vigil should choose those selections that best suit the purpose of the vigil. For those who wish to adhere closely to the model provided, the simplest solution is to assemble a vigil made of only two of the four hours provided here. Others will wish to pick and choose among the many options in order to produce the appropriate rhythm of prayer. Do not, however, let yourself be overwhelmed by the material provided. Use it only as a starting point; let God use the silence to work in you and through you.

If there are to be speakers, their talks may be inserted following the prayer in each of the numbered segments. In order to prevent the talks from disrupting the established, recurring rhythm of the other elements, you may wish to schedule as many short talks as there are segments. Hymn singing also may be included (after the speaker). Such a plan may mean there is time only for four or five segments, each including a cycle of reading, psalm, prayer, speaker, hymn; this may mean dispensing with the larger division of hours (i.e., several sets of these segments) altogether.

As discussed above in the notes for A Vigil in the Presence of God, the leader of the vigil begins prayers by saying, "Let us pray" or "Let us pray the following prayer together." Psalms are similarly introduced. Segment themes may be introduced by the leader as well (these may also be projected overhead). Readers announce each reading as indicated and keep the silence appropriately after the reading, indicating that the silence is over by proclaiming the epigram that follows the rubric "Silence."

a vigil for peace and justice

FIRST HOUR: The Presence of God

To produce materials easily for the First Hour of A Vigil for Peace and Justice, use the caption above as a replacement for the caption for A Vigil in the Presence of God.

SECOND HOUR: The Peace of God

This block of material for prayer and meditation centers attention on the theme of peace. Begin with prayer, then read one or more of the passages provided. Spend most of your time in silence: waiting, listening, using the Jesus Prayer or any other centering devices you find useful.

Prayer

God of peace,
you have taught us
that, in returning and rest, we will be saved
and that, in quietness and confidence,
we will find our strength;
lift us now by the power of your Holy Spirit to your presence,
where we may be still and know that you are God.
You keep in perfect peace
those whose minds are set on you.

You, O God, are in our midst,
and we are called by your name;
to those who receive you,
who are called by your name,
you give power to become children of God.
Enable us to be peacemakers
who will be called children of God;
help us to become your children.

God of Peace,
you have taught us
    that those who take the sword will perish by the sword;
through your prophets, you gave us a vision of the peaceable kingdom
    in which the nations will put down their weapons,
    in which the wolf will lie down with the lamb,
    and a little child shall lead them,
    and none will hurt or destroy in all your holy mountain;
you have given us also a vision of a heavenly city
    whose gates are always open
    and in which are planted trees
    whose leaves are for the healing of the nations;
guide us now by the light of that vision
    to know the things that belong to our peace,
    so that our lives may reflect it
    and our actions establish it
    and our prayers enable us
    to be your servants
    in times of tension
    and places of conflict,
    seeking peace
    and making peace
    and being at peace
    with ourselves
    and with you
    and with all people.

We pray for peace
    among Christians
        in local congregations,
        in national churches,
        in the ecumenical movement;
    among those who work for justice,
        those who work for peace;
    among all people of faith;
    among the nations
        in places of tension and conflict,
        in international counsels and conferences,
        in the United Nations;

we pray for the beating of swords into plowshares
          and spears into pruning hooks,
          for the day when war shall be no more
          and when all hatred shall cease.
Your will is our peace.

Almighty God, whose will is our peace:
    guide the nations of the world into the way of justice and truth,
    and establish among us that peace which is the fruit of righteousness,
    that Christ may rule in all places and in every heart. Amen.

I. GOD'S PROMISE OF PEACE

A Reading from the Prophet Isaiah

A child has been born for us, a son given to us; authority rests upon his shoulders; and he is named Wonderful Counselor, Mighty God, Everlasting Father, Prince of Peace. His authority shall grow continually, and there shall be endless peace for the throne of David and his kingdom. He will establish and uphold it with justice and with righteousness from this time onward and forever-more. The zeal of the LORD of hosts will do this.

                                    —Isaiah 9:6–7

Silence.

...He is named...Prince of Peace...

Psalm 122 *Laetatus sum*

    1 I was glad when they said to me, *
       "Let us go to the house of the LORD."

    2 Now our feet are standing *
       within your gates, O Jerusalem.

    3 Jerusalem is built as a city *
       that is at unity with itself;

    4 To which the tribes go up,
       the tribes of the LORD, *
       the assembly of Israel,
       to praise the Name of the LORD.

5 For there are the thrones of judgment, *
   the thrones of the house of David.

6 Pray for the peace of Jerusalem: *
   "May they prosper who love you.

7 Peace be within your walls *
   and quietness within your towers.

8 For my brethren and companions' sake, *
   I pray for your prosperity.

9 Because of the house of the LORD our God, *
   I will seek to do you good."

Prayer

Lord Jesus Christ,
   we long for peace
         and yet peace seems always to elude our grasp
                  and frustrate our best efforts;
   but you are the source of our peace,
         and you give that gift freely to those who come to you;
help us, then, to come to you with greater faithfulness
   and to depend for peace on your gift, not our efforts;
help us, Lord Jesus, to find our peace in you. Amen.

II. THE GIFT OF PEACE

A Reading from the Gospel according to St. John

Peace I leave with you; my peace I give to you. I do not give to you as the world gives. Do not let your hearts be troubled, and do not let them be afraid. You heard me say to you, "I am going away, and I am coming to you." If you loved me, you would rejoice that I am going to the Father, because the Father is greater than I. And now I have told you this before it occurs, so that when it does occur, you may believe. I will no longer talk much with you, for the ruler of this world is coming. He has no power over me; but I do as the Father has commanded me, so that the world may know that I love the Father.... The hour is coming, indeed it has come, when you will be scattered, each one to his home, and you will leave me alone. Yet I am not alone because the Father is with me. I have said this to you, so that in me you may have peace. In the world you face persecution. But take courage; I have conquered the world!

—John 14:27–31; 16:32–33

Silence.

<h1 align="center">...my peace I give to you...</h1>

Psalm 46 *Deus noster refugium*

1 God is our refuge and strength, *
a very present help in trouble.

2 Therefore we will not fear, though the earth be moved, *
and though the mountains be toppled into the
depths of the sea;

3 Though its waters rage and foam, *
and though the mountains tremble at its tumult.

4 The LORD of hosts is with us; *
the God of Jacob is our stronghold.

5 There is a river whose streams make glad the city of God, *
the holy habitation of the Most High.

6 God is in the midst of her;
she shall not be overthrown; *
God shall help her at the break of day.

7 The nations make much ado, and the kingdoms are shaken; *
God has spoken, and the earth shall melt away.

8 The LORD of hosts is with us; *
the God of Jacob is our stronghold.

9 Come now and look upon the works of the LORD, *
what awesome things he has done on earth.

10 It is he who makes war to cease in all the world; *
he breaks the bow, and shatters the spear,
and burns the shields with fire.

11 "Be still, then, and know that I am God; *
I will be exalted among the nations;
I will be exalted in the earth."

12 The LORD of hosts is with us; *
the God of Jacob is our stronghold.

Prayer

O God, you are peace everlasting,
whose chosen reward is the gift of peace,
and you have taught us that the peacemakers are your children.
Pour your grace into our souls,
that everything discordant may utterly vanish,
and all that makes for peace be sweet to us for ever;
through Jesus Christ our Lord. Amen.

—Charles Kingsley, as quoted in Lenten Prayers for Everyman, *Morehouse-Barlow, 1967, p. 57*

III. THE PEACE OF THE RISEN CHRIST

A Reading from the Gospel according to St. John

When it was evening on that day, the first day of the week, Jesus came and stood among them and said, "Peace be with you." After he said this, he showed them his hands and his side. Then the disciples rejoiced when they saw the Lord. Jesus said to them again, "Peace be with you. As the Father has sent me, so I send you." When he had said this, he breathed on them and said to them, "Receive the Holy Spirit. If you forgive the sins of any, they are forgiven them; if you retain the sins of any, they are retained." But Thomas (who was called the Twin), one of the twelve, was not with them when Jesus came. So the other disciples told him, "We have seen the Lord." But he said to them, "Unless I see the mark of the nails in his hands, and put my finger in the mark of the nails and my hand in his side, I will not believe." A week later his disciples were again in the house, and Thomas was with them. Although the doors were shut, Jesus came and stood among them and said, "Peace be with you." Then he said to Thomas, "Put your finger here and see my hands. Reach out your hand and put it in my side. Do not doubt but believe." Thomas answered him, "My Lord and my God!" Jesus said to him, "Have you believed because you have seen me? Blessed are those who have not seen and yet have come to believe."

—John 20:19–29

Silence.

...Peace be with you...

Psalm 33:1–9, 12–15, 18–22 *Exultate, justi*

1 Rejoice in the LORD, you righteous; *
   it is good for the just to sing praises.

2 Praise the LORD with the harp; *
   play to him upon the psaltery and lyre.

3 Sing for him a new song; *
   sound a fanfare with all your skill upon the trumpet.

4 For the word of the LORD is right, *
   and all his works are sure.

5 He loves righteousness and justice; *
   the loving-kindness of the LORD fills the whole earth.

6 By the word of the LORD were the heavens made, *
   by the breath of his mouth all the heavenly hosts.

7 He gathers up the waters of the ocean as in a waterskin *
   and stores up the depths of the sea.

8 Let all the earth fear the LORD; *
   let all who dwell in the world stand in awe of him.

9 For he spoke, and it came to pass; *
   he commanded, and it stood fast.

12 Happy is the nation whose God is the LORD! *
   happy the people he has chosen to be his own!

13 The LORD looks down from heaven, *
   and beholds all the people in the world.

14 From where he sits enthroned he turns his gaze *
   on all who dwell on the earth.

15 He fashions all the hearts of them *
   and understands all their works.

18 Behold, the eye of the LORD is upon those who fear him, *
   on those who wait upon his love,

19 To pluck their lives from death, *
   and to feed them in time of famine.

20 Our soul waits for the LORD; *
   he is our help and our shield.

21 Indeed, our heart rejoices in him, *
   for in his holy Name we put our trust.

22 Let your loving-kindness, O LORD, be upon us, *
   as we have put our trust in you.

Prayer

O everlasting essence of everything that exists,
   beyond space and time, and yet within them,
   you transcend yet pervade all things:
manifest yourself to us who feel after you,
   seeking you in the shadows of our ignorance.
Stretch forth your hand to help us,
   for we cannot come to you without your aid.
Reveal yourself to us for we seek nothing but you;
   through Jesus Christ our Lord. Amen.

—*Duns Scotus Erigena, as quoted in* 2000 Years of Prayer,
compiled by Michael Counsell, Morehouse Publishing, 1999, p. 85

IV. THE PROCLAIMING OF PEACE

A Reading from the Letter to the Ephesians

Remember that you were once without Christ, being aliens from the commonwealth of Israel, and strangers to the covenants of promise, having no hope and without God in the world. But now in Christ Jesus you who once were far off have been brought near by the blood of Christ. For he is our peace; in his flesh he has made both groups into one and has broken down the dividing wall, that is, the hostility between us. He has abolished the law with its commandments and ordinances, that he might create in himself one new humanity in place of the two, thus making peace, and might reconcile both groups to God in one body through the cross, thus putting to death that hostility through it. So he came and proclaimed peace to you who were far off and peace to those who were near; for through him both of us have access in one Spirit to the Father. So then you are no longer strangers and aliens, but you are citizens with the saints and also members of the household of God, built upon the foundation of the apostles and prophets, with Christ Jesus himself as the cornerstone. In him the whole structure is joined together and grows into a holy temple in the Lord; in whom you also are built together spiritually into a dwelling place for God.... Make every effort to maintain the unity of the Spirit in the bond of peace.

—Ephesians 2:12–22; 4:3

Silence.

...he is our peace...

A Hymn of Peace

> They cast their nets in Galilee
> just off the hills of brown;
> such happy, simple fisher-folk,
> before the Lord came down.
>
> Contented, peaceful fishermen
> before they ever knew
> the peace of God that filled their hearts
> brimful, and broke them too.
>
> Young John who trimmed the flapping sail,
> homeless, in Patmos died.
> Peter, who hauled the teeming net,
> head-down was crucified.
>
> The peace of God, it is no peace,
> but strife closed in the sod.
> Yet let us pray for but one thing—
> the marvelous peace of God.

—William Alexander Percy (1885–1942)
Hymn #661, The Hymnal 1982
Church Publishing Incorporated

Prayer

> O good Jesus,
> > Word of the Father,
> > the brightness of the Father's glory,
> > whom angels desire to behold:
> teach us to do your will,
> > that, guided by your good Spirit,
> > we may come to that blessed city
> > > where there is everlasting day
> > > > and all are of one spirit;
> > > where there is certain security
> > > > and secure eternity
> > > > and eternal tranquility
> > > > and quiet felicity
> > > > and happy sweetness
> > > > and sweet pleasantness;
> > > where you, with the Father and the Holy Spirit,
> > > > are alive and reign,
> > > > one God for ever and ever. Amen.

V. The Ground of Our Peace

A Reading from Julian of Norwich

Thus saw I that God is our true peace, and He is our sure keeper when we are ourselves in unpeace, and He continually works to bring us into endless peace. Full preciously our Lord keeps us when it seems to us that we are nearly forsaken and cast away for our sin and because we have deserved it. And because of meekness that we get hereby, we are raised very high in God's sight by His grace, with so great contrition, and also compassion, and true longing to God. Then they are suddenly delivered from sin and from pain, and taken up to bliss, and made even high saints.

By contrition we are made clean, by compassion we are made ready, and by true longing toward God we are made worthy. These are three means, as I understand, by which all souls come to heaven: that is to say, that have been sinners in earth and shall be saved: for by these three medicines it is possible that every soul be healed.

But our courteous Lord does not will that His servants despair, for often nor for grievous falling: for our falling does not hinder him from loving us. Peace and love are always in us, being and working; but we are not always in peace and in love. But he wills that we take heed thus that He is Ground of all our whole life in love; and furthermore that He is our everlasting keeper and mightily defends us against our enemies.

—*from* The Revelation of Divine Love, *Julian of Norwich*

Silence.

...He is our everlasting keeper...

Psalm 20 *Exaudiat te Dominus*

1 May the LORD answer you in the day of trouble, *
   the Name of the God of Jacob defend you;

2 Send you help from his holy place *
   and strengthen you out of Zion;

3 Remember all your offerings *
   and accept your burnt sacrifice;

4 Grant you your heart's desire *
   and prosper all your plans.

5 We will shout for joy at your victory
   and triumph in the Name of our God; *
   may the LORD grant all your requests.

6 Now I know that the LORD gives victory to his anointed; *
   he will answer him out of his holy heaven,
   with the victorious strength of his right hand.

7 Some put their trust in chariots and some in horses, *
   but we will call upon the Name of the LORD our God.

8 They collapse and fall down, *
   but we will arise and stand upright.

9 O LORD, give victory to the king *
   and answer us when we call.

Prayer

O most loving Father,
you will us to give thanks for all things,
>   to dread nothing but the loss of your presence,
>   and to cast all our care on you,
>>   because you care for us;
preserve us from faithless fears and worldly anxieties,
>   and grant that no clouds of this mortal life
>   may hide from us the light of that immortal love
>   which you have shown us in the face of Jesus Christ,
>>   who is your Son and our Savior,
>>   and in whose Name we pray. Amen.

—The Book of Common Prayer, pp. 216–217, alt.

THIRD HOUR: The Justice of God

The prayer and meditation for the third hour center on the justice of God: recalling God's care for those in need and God's call to the church to work for justice. Begin with prayer, then read one or more of the passages provided. Spend the remainder of the time in silence: waiting, listening, using the Jesus Prayer or any other centering devices you find useful.

Prayer

So near are you to every human life, Eternal God,
>   that you see the misery of your people
>   and hear the cry of the oppressed
>   and know their suffering
>   and send your servants
>   to make known your will for justice
>   and to work for freedom and opportunity for all;
you sent Moses to lead your people
>   and opened the sea before them
>   and went before them night and day in fire and cloud
>   until they came to the land of promise;
you called the prophet Amos
>   to speak to those at ease in Zion
>   and denounce those who oppress the poor and crush the needy
>   and to call for justice to roll down like a mighty flood;

you showed us in Jesus
  a justice which sat down with the poor and the outcast
  and blessed those who thirst for righteousness
  and prayed for forgiveness for those who crucified him;
  and we have promised in our baptism
  to strive for justice and peace among all people
  and to respect the dignity of every human being;
guide us, we pray, as we seek for justice
  so that we may see injustice through your eyes
  and make no compromise with evil;
fill us with your Holy Spirit
  so that we may find words to condemn injustice
  and means to overcome it;
empower us by that same Spirit
  to work with patience and faithfulness,
  wisdom and courage
  until your will is done on earth as it is in heaven.

Let justice be done, Almighty Ruler of the earth,
  wherever people are enslaved
          by force of arms,
          by economic injustice,
          by unjust laws,
          by poverty,
          by fear;
  wherever human life is impoverished
          by lack of food and clothes and shelter,
          by lack of medicine and education,
          by lack of opportunity,
          by prejudice, hatred, and violence.

Let the time be near,
  which your prophet foretold
  and for which we pray
  and for which all people long,
  when the earth shall be filled with the knowledge of God
  and your rule shall be established on earth as it is in heaven. Amen.

I. God's Demand for Justice

A Reading from the Prophet Amos

Seek the LORD and live, or he will break out against the house of Joseph like fire, and it will devour Bethel, with no one to quench it. Ah, you that turn justice to wormwood, and bring righteousness to the ground! The one who made the Pleiades and Orion, and turns deep darkness into the morning, and darkens the day into night, who calls for the waters of the sea, and pours them out on the surface of the earth, the LORD is his name, who makes destruction flash out against the strong, so that destruction comes upon the fortress. They hate the one who reproves in the gate, and they abhor the one who speaks the truth. Therefore because you trample on the poor and take from them levies of grain, you have built houses of hewn stone, but you shall not live in them; you have planted pleasant vineyards, but you shall not drink their wine. For I know how many are your transgressions, and how great are your sins—you who afflict the righteous, who take a bribe, and push aside the needy in the gate. Therefore the prudent will keep silent in such a time; for it is an evil time. Seek good and not evil, that you may live; and so the LORD, the God of hosts, will be with you, just as you have said. Hate evil and love good, and establish justice in the gate; it may be that the LORD, the God of hosts, will be gracious to the remnant of Joseph.... But let justice roll down like waters, and righteousness like an ever-flowing stream.

—*Amos 5:6–15, 24*

Silence.

...establish justice...

Psalm 72 *Deus, judicium*

1 Give the King your justice, O God, *
   and your righteousness to the King's Son;

2 That he may rule your people righteously *
   and the poor with justice;

3 That the mountains may bring prosperity to the people, *
   and the little hills bring righteousness.

4 He shall defend the needy among the people; *
   he shall rescue the poor and crush the oppressor.

5 He shall live as long as the sun and moon endure, *
   from one generation to another.

6 He shall come down like rain upon the mown field, *
   like showers that water the earth.

7 In his time shall the righteous flourish; *
   there shall be abundance of peace
           till the moon shall be no more.

8 He shall rule from sea to sea, *
   and from the River to the ends of the earth.

9 His foes shall bow down before him, *
   and his enemies lick the dust.

10 The kings of Tarshish and of the isles shall pay tribute, *
   and the kings of Arabia and Saba offer gifts.

11 All kings shall bow down before him, *
   and all the nations do him service.

12 For he shall deliver the poor who cries out in distress, *
   and the oppressed who has no helper.

13 He shall have pity on the lowly and poor; *
   he shall preserve the lives of the needy.

14 He shall redeem their lives from oppression and violence, *
   and dear shall their blood be in his sight.

15 Long may he live!
   and may there be given to him gold from Arabia; *
   may prayer be made for him always,
   and may they bless him all the day long.

16 May there be abundance of grain on the earth,
   growing thick even on the hilltops; *
   may its fruit flourish like Lebanon,
   and its grain like grass upon the earth.

17 May his Name remain for ever
   and be established as long as the sun endures; *
   may all the nations bless themselves in him
           and call him blessed.

18 Blessed be the Lord GOD, the God of Israel, *
   who alone does wondrous deeds!

19 And blessed be his glorious Name for ever! *
   and may all the earth be filled with his glory.
   Amen. Amen.

Prayer

Behold, O Lord God, our strivings after a truer and more abiding order.
Give us visions that bring back a lost glory to the earth,
and dreams that foreshadow the better order which you have prepared for us.
Scatter every excuse of frailty and unworthiness:
   consecrate us all with a heavenly mission:
   open to us a clearer prospect of our work.
Give us strength according to our day
   gladly to welcome and gratefully to fulfill it;
   through Jesus Christ our Lord. Amen.

—Brooke Foss Westcott, from 2000 Years of Prayer,
compiled by Michael Counsell, Morehouse Publishing, p. 371

II. GOD WILL BE THE JUDGE

A Reading from the Letter to the Romans

We do not live to ourselves, and we do not die to ourselves. If we live, we live to the Lord, and if we die, we die to the Lord; so then, whether we live or whether we die, we are the Lord's. For to this end Christ died and lived again, so that he might be Lord of both the dead and the living. Why do you pass judgment on your brother or sister? Or you, why do you despise your brother or sister? For we will all stand before the judgment seat of God.... Let us then pursue what makes for peace and for mutual upbuilding.

—Romans 14:7–10, 19

Silence.

...*pursue peace*...

Psalm 111 *Confitebor tibi*

1 Hallelujah!
   I will give thanks to the LORD with my whole heart, *
   in the assembly of the upright, in the congregation.

2 Great are the deeds of the LORD! *
   they are studied by all who delight in them.

3 His work is full of majesty and splendor, *
   and his righteousness endures for ever.

4 He makes his marvelous works to be remembered; *
   the LORD is gracious and full of compassion.

5 He gives food to those who fear him; *
   he is ever mindful of his covenant.

6 He has shown his people the power of his works *
   in giving them the lands of the nations.

7 The works of his hands are faithfulness and justice; *
   all his commandments are sure.

8 They stand fast for ever and ever, *
   because they are done in truth and equity.

9 He sent redemption to his people;
   he commanded his covenant for ever; *
   holy and awesome is his Name.

10 The fear of the LORD is the beginning of wisdom; *
   those who act accordingly have a good understanding;
   his praise endures for ever.

Prayer

You alone, O Lord our God,
   know us within and without;
   you know the thoughts and intentions
   that lie behind our actions.
You alone, O Lord our God,
   are able to be our judge:
   to weigh what we have done
   and what others have done
   and to establish justice among us.

Let us then seek only to serve
    the cause of your justice
and not our own,
      that all things may lead to the peace
      which comes from justice
      and which you alone can give. Amen.

III. GOD'S JUSTICE

A Reading from the Gospel according to St. Matthew

Jesus said, "When the Son of Man comes in his glory, and all the angels with him, then he will sit on the throne of his glory. All the nations will be gathered before him, and he will separate people one from another as a shepherd separates the sheep from the goats, and he will put the sheep at his right hand and the goats at the left. Then the king will say to those at his right hand, 'Come, you that are blessed by my Father, inherit the kingdom prepared for you from the foundation of the world; for I was hungry and you gave me food, I was thirsty and you gave me something to drink, I was a stranger and you welcomed me, I was naked and you gave me clothing, I was sick and you took care of me, I was in prison and you visited me.' Then the righteous will answer him, 'Lord, when was it that we saw you hungry and gave you food, or thirsty and gave you something to drink? And when was it that we saw you a stranger and welcomed you, or naked and gave you clothing? And when was it that we saw you sick or in prison and visited you?' And the king will answer them, 'Truly I tell you, just as you did it to one of the least of these who are members of my family, you did it to me.' Then he will say to those at his left hand, 'You that are accursed, depart from me into the eternal fire prepared for the devil and his angels; for I was hungry and you gave me no food, I was thirsty and you gave me nothing to drink, I was a stranger and you did not welcome me, naked and you did not give me clothing, sick and in prison and you did not visit me.' Then they also will answer, 'Lord, when was it that we saw you hungry or thirsty or a stranger or naked or sick or in prison, and did not take care of you?' Then he will answer them, 'Truly I tell you, just as you did not do it to one of the least of these, you did not do it to me.' And these will go away into eternal punishment, but the righteous into eternal life."

—*Matthew 25:31–46*

Silence.

...when was it that we saw you?

A Hymn of God's Justice

Judge eternal, throned in splendor,
Lord of lords and King of kings,
with thy living fire of judgment
purge this land of bitter things;
solace all its wide dominion
with the healing of thy wings.

Crown, O God, thine own endeavor;
cleave our darkness with thy sword;
feed all those who do not know thee
with the richness of thy word;
cleanse the body of this nation
through the glory of the Lord.

—Henry Scott Holland (1847–1918)
Hymn #596, stanzas 1,2, The Hymnal 1982
Church Publishing Incorporated

Prayer

We will stand before you, O Lord, at the last,
   and we will know as we are known,
   and we will see what we have failed to see;
open our eyes to see and know
   that we stand in your presence now,
   that you are here before us
         in the needs of family, friends, and strangers alike,
         seeking our response of love;
grant that we may respond now in such a way
   that we may be prepared to stand before you at the last. Amen.

IV. THE VISION OF JUSTICE

A Reading from *The Things that Remain* by William Ralph Inge

The vision of the City of God is a vision of reality, but it is a vision, not knowledge—not knowledge of that which "eye hath not seen, nor ear heard, nor hath entered into the heart of man to conceive." The light that it shed on our dark earth is a somewhat fitful light. We pray, "Thy will be done in earth as it is in heaven." We believe that it will be done. We even believe, though it is a hard saying, that all things will work together for good to those who love God. But when we descend to the particular, and encourage ourselves by saying the cause

43

of justice and humanity cannot be defeated because there is a heaven above us, when we use the words of the Old Testament promising victory and prosperity to the righteous, we are forgetting the lessons of history, which show us a great shadow lying right across the earth—it is the shadow of the cross. In our very deepest heart of hearts we would not have it otherwise. We are called to be under the banner of the crucified.

And so we look for another country, that is, a heavenly, and yet we know that even in the cloudy and dark day this earth of ours is no derelict outcast of God's creation, but that part of heaven where our lot is cast, a world marred, but a world redeemed, through which we walk by faith, not having received the promises, but beholding them afar off, and remembering the words of St. Paul, that the object for which Jesus Christ ascended up far above all heavens was not to leave us comfortless, but that He might fill all things.

—William Ralph Inge, The Things that Remain, *Harper and Brothers, 1958, p. 16*

Silence.

...a vision of reality...

Psalm 82:1, 5–8 *Deus stetit*

> 1 God takes his stand in the council of heaven; *
> he gives judgment in the midst of the gods:

> 4 "Rescue the weak and the poor;
> deliver them from the power of thewicked

> 5 They do not know, neither do they understand;
> they go about in darkness; *
> all the foundations of the earth are shaken.

> 6 Now I say to you, 'You are gods, *
> and all of you children of the Most High;

> 7 Nevertheless, you shall die like mortals, *
> and fall like any prince.'"

> 8 Arise, O God, and rule the earth, *
> for you shall take all nations for your own.

Prayer

Almighty God, you have created us in your own image; grant us grace fearlessly to contend against evil and to make no peace with oppression; and, that we may reverently use our freedom, help us to employ it in the maintenance of justice among all people to the glory of your Name; through Jesus Christ our Lord. Amen.

—The Book of Common Prayer, 1928, p. 44, alt.

FOURTH HOUR: The Mercy of God

The fourth hour of material for prayer and meditation is centered on the healing power of God for reconciliation: recalling God's mercy to all people through the ages, offering ourselves as instruments of that mercy, giving thanks for the healing without which life would be without hope. Begin with prayer, then read one or more of the passages provided. Spend the remainder of the time in silence: waiting, listening, using the Jesus Prayer or any other centering devices you find useful.

Prayer

Waiting at the foot of your cross, Lord Christ,
    we pray for healing and reconciliation
    in your world and in your church;
our sins weigh us down;
    they divide us;
    they set us in warring camps;
    they blind us so we cannot see the way of peace;
    they deafen us so we cannot hear the word of healing;
    they fill us with faithless fears,
        not only of our enemies
        but of our neighbors;
        even of ourselves;
forgive us, have mercy on us,
    turn our hearts toward your love,
    open our hearts to your peace,
    fill our hearts with your holy and life-giving Spirit;
grant that we may go out to serve you,
    forgiven, strengthened, and renewed;

make us willing to sacrifice our own imagined interests,
    to spend and not to count the cost,
    to share your suffering without complaint,
    to seek no victories for ourselves
            but only for others
            and for your love's sake.
Give us, eternal God,
    the gift of healing and renewal;
where there is need,
    let us share the gifts you have given us;
where there is anger,
    let us bear witness to your patience,
    let us share your suffering;
    let us hold up the vision of your peace;
where there is conflict,
    let us be present in your Name
            to bind up wounds,
            to offer the gift of understanding,
            and to seek your will;
your will, not our own,
here on this earth, now, and among all people. Amen.

I. CHRIST SUFFERS FOR US

A Reading from the Prophet Isaiah

He was despised and rejected by others; a man of suffering and acquainted with infirmity; and as one from whom others hide their faces he was despised, and we held him of no account. Surely he has borne our infirmities and carried our diseases; yet we accounted him stricken, struck down by God, and afflicted. But he was wounded for our transgressions, crushed for our iniquities; upon him was the punishment that made us whole, and by his bruises we are healed. All we like sheep have gone astray; we have all turned to our own way, and the Lord has laid on him the iniquity of us all.

—*Isaiah 53:3–6*

Silence.

...by his bruises we are healed...

Psalm 85 *Benedixisti, Domine*

1 You have been gracious to your land, O LORD, *
   you have restored the good fortune of Jacob.

2 You have forgiven the iniquity of your people *
   and blotted out all their sins.

3 You have withdrawn all your fury *
   and turned yourself from your wrathful indignation.

4 Restore us then, O God our Savior; *
   let your anger depart from us.

5 Will you be displeased with us for ever? *
   will you prolong your anger from age to age?

6 Will you not give us life again, *
   that your people may rejoice in you?

7 Show us your mercy, O LORD, *
   and grant us your salvation.

8 I will listen to what the LORD God is saying, *
   for he is speaking peace to his faithful people
   and to those who turn their hearts to him.

9 Truly, his salvation is very near to those who fear him, *
   that his glory may dwell in our land.

10 Mercy and truth have met together; *
    righteousness and peace have kissed each other.

11 Truth shall spring up from the earth, *
    and righteousness shall look down from heaven.

12 The LORD will indeed grant prosperity, *
    and our land will yield its increase.

13 Righteousness shall go before him, *
    and peace shall be a pathway for his feet.

Prayer

Lord, we have turned away from you too often
    and failed to see your face
        in the face of suffering and poverty;
yet you are always merciful
    and spare us when we deserve only wrath;
mold our hearts, Lord,
    and fill them with that same mercy you have showed us,
    that we may be instruments of your peace
        and messengers of your mercy. Amen.

II. A NEW CREATION IN CHRIST

A Reading from the Second Letter to the Corinthians

The love of Christ urges us on, because we are convinced that one has died for all; therefore all have died. And he died for all, so that those who live might live no longer for themselves, but for him who died and was raised for them. From now on, therefore, we regard no one from a human point of view; even though we once knew Christ from a human point of view, we know him no longer in that way. So if anyone is in Christ, there is a new creation: everything old has passed away; see, everything has become new! All this is from God, who reconciled us to himself through Christ, and has given us the ministry of reconciliation; that is, in Christ God was reconciling the world to himself, not counting their trespasses against them, and entrusting the message of reconciliation to us. So we are ambassadors for Christ, since God is making his appeal through us; we entreat you on behalf of Christ, be reconciled to God.

—2 Corinthians 5:14–20

Silence.

...everything has become new!...

A Hymn of God's Mercy

There's a wideness in God's mercy
like the wideness of the sea;
there's a kindness in his justice,
which is more than liberty.
There is welcome for the sinner,
and more graces for the good;
there is mercy with the Savior;
there is healing in his blood.

For the love of God is broader
than the measure of the mind;
and the heart of the eternal
is most wonderfully kind.
If our love were but more faithful,
we should take him at his word;
and our life would be thanksgiving
for the goodness of the Lord.

—Frederick William Faber (1814–1863)
Hymn #469–470, The Hymnal 1982
Church Publishing Incorporated

III. GOD'S PROMISE FULFILLED IN CHRIST

A Reading from the Gospel according to St. Luke

John summoned two of his disciples and sent them to the Lord to ask, "Are you the one who is to come, or are we to wait for another?" When the men had come to him, they said, "John the Baptist has sent us to you to ask, 'Are you the one who is to come, or are we to wait for another?'" Jesus had just then cured many people of diseases, plagues, and evil spirits, and had given sight to many who were blind. And he answered them, "Go and tell John what you have seen and heard: the blind receive their sight, the lame walk, the lepers are cleansed, the deaf hear, the dead are raised, the poor have good news brought to them. And blessed is anyone who takes no offense at me."

—Luke 7:18–23

Silence.

...tell...what you have seen and heard...

Psalm 98 *Cantate Domino*

1 Sing to the LORD a new song, *
   for he has done marvelous things.

2 With his right hand and his holy arm *
   has he won for himself the victory.

3 The LORD has made known his victory; *
   his righteousness has he openly shown in
         the sight of the nations.

4 He remembers his mercy and faithfulness to
      the house of Israel, *
and all the ends of the earth have seen the
      victory of our God.

5 Shout with joy to the LORD, all you lands; *
lift up your voice, rejoice, and sing.

6 Sing to the LORD with the harp, *
with the harp and the voice of song.

7 With trumpets and the sound of the horn *
shout with joy before the King, the LORD.

8 Let the sea make a noise and all that is in it, *
the lands and those who dwell therein.

9 Let the rivers clap their hands, *
and let the hills ring out with joy before the LORD,
when he comes to judge the earth.

10 In righteousness shall he judge the world *
and the peoples with equity.

Prayer

When John's disciples came to you, Lord Jesus,
    you told them to go and tell John what they had seen and heard;
    help us also to tell our friends and neighbors
        what we have seen and heard;
    help us to sing your praise
        so that all lands may rejoice in your goodness
           and glorify your Name. Amen.

IV. IRRESISTIBLE GRACE

A Reading from *The Man on a Donkey* by H. F. M. Prescott

Once he had seen his sin as a thing that clung close as his shadow clung to his heels; now he knew that it was the very stuff of his soul. Never could he, a leaking bucket not to he mended, retain God's saving Grace, however freely out-poured. Never could he, that heavy lump of sin do any other than sink, and sink again, however often Christ, walking on the waves, should stretch His hand to lift and bring him safe. He did not know that though the bucket be leaky it matters not at all when it is deep in the deep sea, and the water both without it and within. He did not know, because he was too proud to know, that a man must endure to sink, and sink again, but always crying upon God, never for shame ceasing to cry, until the day when he shall find himself lifted by the bland swell of that power, inward, secret, as little to be known as to be doubted, the power of omnipotent grace in tranquil irresistible operation.

—*H. F. M. Prescott,* The Man on a Donkey

Silence.

...always crying upon God...

Psalm 150 *Laudate Dominum*

  1 Hallelujah!
     Praise God in his holy temple; *
     praise him in the firmament of his power.

  2 Praise him for his mighty acts; *
     praise him for his excellent greatness.

  3 Praise him with the blast of the ram's-horn; *
     praise him with lyre and harp.

  4 Praise him with timbrel and dance; *
     praise him with strings and pipe.

  5 Praise him with resounding cymbals; *
     praise him with loud-clanging cymbals.

  6 Let everything that has breath *
     praise the LORD.
     Hallelujah!

CLOSING PRAYERS

Psalm 130:4–7 *De profundis*

4 I wait for the LORD; my soul waits for him; *
   in his word is my hope.

5 My soul waits for the LORD,
   more than watchmen for the morning, *
   more than watchmen for the morning.

6 O Israel, wait for the LORD, *
   for with the LORD there is mercy;

7 With him there is plenteous redemption, *
   and he shall redeem Israel from all their sins. Amen.

A Collect for the Renewal of Life

O God, the King eternal, whose light divides the day from the night and turns the shadow of death into the morning: Drive far from us all wrong desires, incline our hearts to keep your law, and guide our feet into the way of peace; that, having done your will with cheerfulness during the day, we may, when night comes, rejoice to give you thanks; through Jesus Christ our Lord. Amen.

—The Book of Common Prayer, p. 99

For the Church

Gracious Father, we pray for your holy Catholic Church. Fill it with all truth, in all truth with all peace. Where it is corrupt, purify it; where it is in error, direct it; where in any thing it is amiss, reform it. Where it is right, strengthen it; where it is in want, provide for it; where it is divided, reunite it; for the sake of Jesus Christ your Son our Savior. Amen.

—The Book of Common Prayer, p. 816, alt.

For Clergy and People

Almighty and everlasting God, from whom comes every good and perfect gift: Send down upon our bishops, and other clergy, and upon the congregations committed to their charge, the healthful Spirit of your grace; and, that they may truly please you, pour upon them the continual dew of your blessing. Grant this, O Lord, for the honor of our Advocate and Mediator, Jesus Christ. Amen.

—The Book of Common Prayer, p. 817, alt.

~

a vigil
for the
sick

~

NOTES FOR
a vigil for the sick

In the first English Prayer Book of 1549, Thomas Cranmer, the Archbishop of Canterbury, included an "Office for the Visitation of the Sick" and instructed that the priest should "address the sick person on the use and meaning of sickness." That is a phrase on which to meditate. It suggests that the proper Christian response to illness is not only to consult a doctor, or simply to pray for healing, but to consider what use can be made of the time of ill health. A vigil in time of sickness, then, should be concerned as much with discerning God's will as with asking God to respond to our will. God's will is for our good, but our good can sometimes be accomplished through times of sickness and even through suffering. Suffering—as the cross at the center of our faith reminds us—is not purely negative; it can be powerfully used for God's purposes and for human good.

Vigils kept in time of sickness can be large, public events or they can be "private" (a few people keeping vigil together or "in turns" one or two at a time). The private format is the more usual, probably because such vigils can be put together quickly on behalf of someone who is critically ill or facing surgery. Private vigils sometimes are kept in churches or chapels but are equally likely to take place in hospital waiting rooms, at bedsides, or even in homes.

For private vigils

The material provided here is arranged for use by those keeping a private vigil. The major themes are: the faith and trust with which we come to God; God's use of suffering; our ability to share or bear another's suffering; and our need to enter into and share the suffering of Christ for all humanity.

The material is arranged into three large sections or "hours," each of which begins with a prayer followed by three segments composed of a reading, a time of silence, a psalm, and a prayer. Move through the readings, psalms, and prayers slowly and meditatively so that they blend easily with the more important times of silent prayer and silent waiting on God.

It is suggested that at least twenty minutes be spent with each segment. If an individual is taking part in the vigil for one hour, she/he might use the first hour or choose three blocks of material, preferably in the order given here (for example segment one of the first hour, segment three of the second hour, and segment two of the third hour). The person or persons organizing the vigil, however, might ask those participating to use the segments in order. The Closing Prayer at the very end of the vigil may be used by any and all participants, regardless of the material they have been assigned.

Candles may be used by the various keepers of the vigil as a liturgical way of marking their participation. See the notes for A Vigil in the Presence of God.

For public vigils

Public vigils may range from small gatherings in parish chapels that feel almost as intimate and informal as private vigils all the way up to formal, rehearsed liturgies that pack the parish church. Some public vigils—for example a vigil that is kept when several neighborhood firefighters have been injured on duty—may need to be expanded beyond the parish level to the municipal level. Such vigils may require a space that is larger than the local church—a concert hall or a school auditorium. The planning process for community-wide vigils usually includes civic leaders and civil authorities, some of whom may wish to include their own thoughts and meditations in the roster of readings, silences, psalms, and prayers; schedule speakers after the prayer that concludes each segment; a hymn may follow the speaker. Sometimes the music, prayers, and readings from several Christian traditions are combined to create a service with wider, more ecumenical appeal; or vigil planners may determine that an interfaith service will best serve their community. Many of the prayers included here are specifically Christian and even specifically Anglican, but careful, practiced liturgy planners can use these models to create a service that is appropriate to the circumstances and the participants.

The leader of a public Vigil for the Sick begins prayers by saying, "Let us pray" (if the leader is to pray aloud on behalf of the assembly) or "Let us pray the following prayer together" (if the assembly is to join in). Before each psalm, the leader says, "Let us read Psalm [number] together"; or, "Let us read Psalm [number] responsively" (if you plan to read responsively, and if your service is a large ecumenical one, you may want to put the congregational responses in boldface). Readers announce each reading as indicated. After the reading, the reader remains in place, keeping the silence for the appropriate amount of time. The silence concludes when the reader proclaims the brief, epigraphic echo from the previous reading; these appear in the vigil text immediately after the rubric "Silence." If you chose to retain recognizable thematic segments in your vigil, have the leader announce them to the assembly (see notes for a Vigil in the Presence of God for examples); or you may wish to use an overhead projector to flash thematic titles before the assembly at the appropriate time.

Outline of a public Vigil for the Sick

1. The vigil may begin with Compline, Evening Prayer, a time of silence, an entrance hymn, or a brief call to prayer.
2. Materials from A Vigil for the Sick may then be used, alternating readings with psalms or hymns and including extended times of silent prayer. Selections from A Vigil in the Presence of God also are appropriate.
3. The vigil may conclude with a celebration of the Eucharist.

a vigil for the sick

FIRST HOUR: Waiting in Faithfulness and Trust

Prayer

> In you alone, O God, we live and move and have our being;
>> your Holy Spirit breathes life into us
>>> moment by moment and day by day;
>> therefore, we wait for your loving-kindness, O God,
>>> and open our hearts to your presence,
>>> asking that you be with us now
>>> and hold us in your strengthening care;
>> help us to put away all the distractions of our daily lives,
>>> to quiet our hearts and our minds,
>>> to seek and to know your presence with us now;
>> and then teach us to wait peacefully in your presence
>>> and to cast all our cares on you because you care for us.
>> Give us, Almighty Creator, the gift of life renewed;
>> grant us, Healing Savior, the gift of life renewed;
>> fill us, Indwelling Spirit, with the gift of life renewed. Amen.

I. THE MYSTERY OF SUFFERING

A Reading from the Book of Job

> Then Job answered:
> "Today also my complaint is bitter;
> his hand is heavy despite my groaning.
> Oh, that I knew where I might find him,
> that I might come even to his dwelling!
> I would lay my case before him,
> and fill my mouth with arguments.
> I would learn what he would answer me,
> and understand what he would say to me.

Would he contend with me in the greatness of his power?
No; but he would give heed to me.
There an upright person could reason with him,
and I should be acquitted forever by my judge.
If I go forward, he is not there;
or backward, I cannot perceive him;
on the left he hides, and I cannot behold him;
I turn to the right, but I cannot see him.
But he knows the way that I take;
when he has tested me, I shall come out like gold.
My foot has held fast to his steps;
I have kept his way and have not turned aside.
I have not departed from the commandment of his lips;
I have treasured in my bosom the words of his mouth.
But he stands alone and who can dissuade him?
What he desires, that he does."

—Job 23:1–13

Silence.

...he knows the way I take...

Psalm 42:1–11, 14–15 *Quemadmodum*

1 As the deer longs for the water-brooks, *
so longs my soul for you, O God.

2 My soul is athirst for God, athirst for the living God; *
when shall I come to appear before the presence of God?

3 My tears have been my food day and night, *
while all day long they say to me,
"Where now is your God?"

4 I pour out my soul when I think on these things: *
how I went with the multitude and led them into the
house of God,

5 With the voice of praise and thanksgiving, *
among those who keep holy-day.

6 Why are you so full of heaviness, O my soul? *
and why are you so disquieted within me?

7 Put your trust in God; *
   for I will yet give thanks to him,
   who is the help of my countenance, and my God.

8 My soul is heavy within me; *
   therefore I will remember you from the land of Jordan,
   and from the peak of Mizar among the heights of Hermon.

9 One deep calls to another in the noise of your cataracts; *
   all your rapids and floods have gone over me.

10 The LORD grants his loving-kindness in the daytime; *
    in the night season his song is with me,
    a prayer to the God of my life.

11 I will say to the God of my strength,
    "Why have you forgotten me? *
    and why do I go so heavily while the enemy oppresses me?"

14 Why are you so full of heaviness, O my soul? *
    and why are you so disquieted within me?

15 Put your trust in God; *
    for I will yet give thanks to him,
    who is the help of my countenance, and my God.

Prayer

O most loving Father,
you will us to give thanks for all things,
   to dread nothing but the loss of your presence,
   and to cast all our care on you,
         because you care for us;
preserve us from faithless fears and worldly anxieties,
   and grant that no clouds of this mortal life
   may hide from us the light of that immortal love
   which you have shown us in the face of Jesus Christ,
         who is your Son and our Savior,
         and in whose Name we pray. Amen.

II. Faithful Waiting

A Reading from the Prophet Habakkuk

I will stand at my watch-post, and station myself on the rampart; I will keep watch to see what he will say to me, and what he will answer concerning my complaint. Then the LORD answered me and said: Write the vision; make it plain on tablets, so that a runner may read it. For there is still a vision for the appointed time; it speaks of the end, and does not lie. If it seems to tarry, wait for it; it will surely come, it will not delay. Though the fig tree does not blossom, and no fruit is on the vines; though the produce of the olive fails and the fields yield no food; though the flock is cut off from the fold and there is no herd in the stalls, yet I will rejoice in the LORD; I will exult in the God of my salvation.

—Habakkuk 2:1–3; 3:17–18

Silence.

...I will stand at my watch-post...

Psalm 25 *Ad te, Domine, levavi*

1 To you, O LORD, I lift up my soul;
   my God, I put my trust in you; *
   let me not be humiliated,
   nor let my enemies triumph over me.

2 Let none who look to you be put to shame; *
   let the treacherous be disappointed in their schemes.

3 Show me your ways, O LORD, *
   and teach me your paths.

4 Lead me in your truth and teach me, *
   for you are the God of my salvation;
   in you have I trusted all the day long.

5 Remember, O LORD, your compassion and love, *
   for they are from everlasting.

6 Remember not the sins of my youth and my transgressions; *
   remember me according to your love
   and for the sake of your goodness, O LORD.

7 Gracious and upright is the LORD; *
   therefore he teaches sinners in his way.

8 He guides the humble in doing right *
and teaches his way to the lowly.

9 All the paths of the LORD are love and faithfulness *
to those who keep his covenant and his testimonies.

10 For your Name's sake, O LORD, *
forgive my sin, for it is great.

11 Who are they who fear the LORD? *
he will teach them the way that they should choose.

12 They shall dwell in prosperity, *
and their offspring shall inherit the land.

13 The LORD is a friend to those who fear him *
and will show them his covenant.

14 My eyes are ever looking to the LORD, *
for he shall pluck my feet out of the net.

15 Turn to me and have pity on me, *
for I am left alone and in misery.

16 The sorrows of my heart have increased; *
bring me out of my troubles.

17 Look upon my adversity and misery *
and forgive me all my sin.

18 Look upon my enemies, for they are many, *
and they bear a violent hatred against me.

19 Protect my life and deliver me; *
let me not be put to shame, for I have trusted in you.

20 Let integrity and uprightness preserve me, *
for my hope has been in you.

21 Deliver Israel, O God, *
out of all his troubles.

Prayer

You have taught us, Lord God,
> that we will be saved by returning and rest,
> that our strength will be found in quietness and confidence;
lift us, then, by the might of your Spirit
>> to your presence
> where we may be still
> and know that you are God. Amen.

–The Book of Common Prayer, 1928, p. 595, alt.

III. Waiting for the Lord

A Reading from the Letter of James

Be patient, beloved, until the coming of the Lord. The farmer waits for the precious crop from the earth, being patient with it until it receives the early and the late rains. You also must be patient. Strengthen your hearts, for the coming of the Lord is near. Beloved, do not grumble against one another, so that you may not be judged. See, the Judge is standing at the doors! As an example of suffering and patience, beloved, take the prophets who spoke in the name of the Lord. Indeed we call blessed those who showed endurance. You have heard of the endurance of Job, and you have seen the purpose of the Lord, how the Lord is compassionate and merciful.

—James 5:7–11

Silence.

...You must be patient...

Psalm 13 *Usquequo, Domine?*

> 1 How long, O LORD?
> will you forget me for ever? *
> how long will you hide your face from me?

> 2 How long shall I have perplexity in my mind,
> and grief in my heart, day after day? *
> how long shall my enemy triumph over me?

> 3 Look upon me and answer me, O LORD my God; *
> give light to my eyes, lest I sleep in death;

4 Lest my enemy say, "I have prevailed over him," *
and my foes rejoice that I have fallen.

5 But I put my trust in your mercy; *
my heart is joyful because of your saving help.

6 I will sing to the Lord, for he has dealt with me richly; *
I will praise the Name of the Lord Most High.

Prayer

Almighty God, the fountain of all wisdom,
you know our needs before we ask,
and you know our ignorance, sometimes, in asking:
have compassion on our weaknesses,
and grant us those good things that,
in our lack of faith, we dare not ask of you and,
in our blindness, cannot ask of you. Amen.

—adapted from the Book of Common Prayer, 1928, pp. 49–50

IV. THE POWER OF PRAYER

A Reading from *The Prayers of Jesus* by Edward Bouverie Pusey

Marvelous among the mysteries of this strange mysterious world, is the mystery of prayer. Mysterious in its simplicity, boundless in its might, endless in its efficacy. It needs no gifts of nature, no knowledge, save the knowledge of God, no spoken words, no plainly conceived thoughts, no cultivation of the mind. The simplest soul, to which God has made Himself known, has a power above all created intellect, reaching where the acutest intelligence loses itself influencing the destinies of its fellowmen, beyond man's mightiest power or his most piercing intelligence. For it is supernatural. Outwardly, it is a few words from the inmost soul, or a deep unspoken longing, darted up, our human soul knows not how, gone so swiftly that we cannot follow it. We seem to have done nothing. If we were in earnest, it gave vent to our soul's deep desire; it may have been for the salvation of souls, for the mitigation of all dishonour to God's holiness, for the staying of the withering unbelief around us, of the wasting of souls for whom Christ died, for the arresting of one single sin, for the gaining of the last grace needed for a soul balancing between sin and God. The prayer has sped. We hear no answer, we see no sign: perhaps until we are in eternity, we shall never know what became of it. But it had an inward power, a Divine might from God to God, a covenanted omnipotency with the Omnipotent. God has pledged His truth, that is, Himself, that if it has been asked according to His will, He will give it.

—*Edward Bouverie Pusey,* The Prayers of Jesus

Silence.

...Prayer has an inward power...

Psalm 143:1–2, 4–11 *Domine, exaudi*

1 LORD, hear my prayer,
 and in your faithfulness heed my supplications; *
 answer me in your righteousness.

2 Enter not into judgment with your servant, *
 for in your sight shall no one living be justified.

4 My spirit faints within me; *
 my heart within me is desolate.

5 I remember the time past;
 I muse upon all your deeds; *
 I consider the works of your hands.

6 I spread out my hands to you; *
 my soul gasps to you like a thirsty land.

7 O LORD, make haste to answer me; my spirit fails me; *
 do not hide your face from me
 or I shall be like those who go down to the Pit.

8 Let me hear of your loving-kindness in the morning,
 for I put my trust in you; *
 show me the road that I must walk,
 for I lift up my soul to you.

10 Teach me to do what pleases you, for you are my God; *
 let your good Spirit lead me on level ground.

11 Revive me, O LORD, for your Name's sake; *
 for your righteousness' sake, bring me out of trouble.

Prayer

> You love surrounds us, good and gracious God;
> > the sun warms the air,
> > the stars sparkle in the evening sky,
> > the sown seed ripens
> > > into the crops that nourish your people;
> help us, Lord God, to know your presence in our lives
> > and your constant care for us,
> that we may praise you in our lives
> > and make known your praise to others. Amen.

SECOND HOUR: God's Use of Suffering

Prayer

> All things work together for good, Lord God,
> > for those who love you;
> you are able to work your will and accomplish our good
> > not only through our success and happiness
> > > but also, when necessary, through suffering and pain;
> you have taught your people
> > through slavery and exile,
> > > and the blood of the martyrs,
> and you have opened the way of life to all the world
> > through the suffering of Jesus
> > > and his death on Calvary's cross;
> you have revealed your power
> > in the endurance of the church in persecution,
> > in the witness of the saints,
> > in the faithfulness of those who are lonely,
> > > handicapped, and frail,
> > > who are yet sustained and upheld by the knowledge
> > > > that your strength is sufficient for us
> > > > and made perfect in our weaknesses.
> Grant us, Almighty and ever-loving God,
> > sufficient strength in our weaknesses
> > > to hold to you alone
> > > at all times
> > > and at this time. Amen.

I. Christ Takes Our Weaknesses upon Himself

A Reading from the Prophet Isaiah

He was despised and rejected by others; a man of suffering and acquainted with infirmity; and as one from whom others hide their faces he was despised, and we held him of no account. Surely he has borne our infirmities and carried our diseases; yet we accounted him stricken, struck down by God, and afflicted. But he was wounded for our transgressions, crushed for our iniquities; upon him was the punishment that made us whole, and by his bruises we are healed. All we like sheep have gone astray; we have all turned to our own way, and the LORD has laid on him the iniquity of us all.

—Isaiah 53:3–6

Silence.

...he has borne our infirmities...

Psalm 27 *Dominus illuminatio*

1 The LORD is my light and my salvation;
   whom then shall I fear? *
   the LORD is the strength of my life;
   of whom then shall I be afraid?

2 When evildoers came upon me to eat up my flesh, *
   it was they, my foes and my adversaries, who
         stumbled and fell.

3 Though an army should encamp against me, *
   yet my heart shall not be afraid;

4 And though war should rise up against me, *
   yet will I put my trust in him.

5 One thing have I asked of the LORD;
   one thing I seek; *
   that I may dwell in the house of the LORD all the days
         of my life;

6 To behold the fair beauty of the LORD *
   and to seek him in his temple.

7 For in the day of trouble he shall keep me safe
        in his shelter; *
  he shall hide me in the secrecy of his dwelling
  and set me high upon a rock.

8 Even now he lifts up my head *
  above my enemies round about me.

9 Therefore I will offer in his dwelling an oblation
  with sounds of great gladness; *
  I will sing and make music to the LORD.

10 Hearken to my voice, O LORD, when I call; *
   have mercy on me and answer me.

11 You speak in my heart and say, "Seek my face." *
   Your face, LORD, will I seek.

12 Hide not your face from me, *
   nor turn away your servant in displeasure.

13 You have been my helper;
   cast me not away; *
   do not forsake me, O God of my salvation.

14 Though my father and my mother forsake me, *
   the LORD will sustain me.

15 Show me your way, O LORD; *
   lead me on a level path, because of my enemies.

16 Deliver me not into the hand of my adversaries, *
   for false witnesses have risen up against me,
   and also those who speak malice.

17 What if I had not believed
   that I should see the goodness of the LORD *
   in the land of the living!

18 O tarry and await the LORD's pleasure;
   be strong, and he shall comfort your heart; *
   wait patiently for the LORD.

Prayer

> Almighty and eternal God,
>> you are a strong tower to those
>>> who turn to you in trust;
>> all things in heaven and earth bow before you;
> be our defense against the forces of evil,
>> and help us know and believe
>>> that there is no other Name under heaven
>> in whom and through whom we may obtain salvation
>> except the Name of your Son, Jesus Christ,
>>> in whose Name we pray. Amen.

II. God's Grace Is Sufficient

A Reading from the Second Letter to the Corinthians

To keep me from being too elated, a thorn was given me in the flesh, a messenger of Satan to torment me, to keep me from being too elated. Three times I appealed to the Lord about this, that it would leave me, but he said to me, "My grace is sufficient for you, for power is made perfect in weakness." So, I will boast all the more gladly of my weaknesses, so that the power of Christ may dwell in me. Therefore I am content with weaknesses, insults, hardships, persecutions, and calamities for the sake of Christ; for whenever I am weak, then I am strong.

—*2 Corinthians 12:7–10*

Silence.

...my grace is sufficient for you...

Psalm 130 *De profundis*

1 Out of the depths have I called to you, O LORD;
LORD, hear my voice; *
let your ears consider well the voice of my supplication.

2 If you, LORD, were to note what is done amiss, *
O LORD, who could stand?

3 For there is forgiveness with you; *
therefore you shall be feared.

4 I wait for the LORD; my soul waits for him; *
in his word is my hope.

5 My soul waits for the LORD,
   more than watchmen for the morning, *
   more than watchmen for the morning.

6 O Israel, wait for the LORD, *
   for with the LORD there is mercy;

7 With him there is plenteous redemption, *
   and he shall redeem Israel from all their sins.

Prayer

Help us, Lord God,
   to find a meaning in suffering:
            let us recognize our need of your strength;
            let us learn your ability to bring good out of evil;
            let us use our weaknesses to learn patience;
            let us wait for you to show us
                     your constant presence
                     and your healing love;
            let us be content, if need be, with weakness,
                     knowing your strength.
Grant that this time of physical weakness
   may be a time of spiritual renewal and growth.
May your will, not ours, be done. Amen.

III. CONSOLATION IN SUFFERING

A Reading from the Second Letter to the Corinthians

Blessed be the God and Father of our Lord Jesus Christ, the Father of mercies and the God of all consolation, who consoles us in all our affliction, so that we may be able to console those who are in any affliction with the consolation with which we ourselves are consoled by God. For just as the sufferings of Christ are abundant for us, so also our consolation is abundant through Christ. If we are being afflicted, it is for your consolation and salvation; if we are being consoled, it is for your consolation, which you experience when you patiently endure the same sufferings that we are also suffering. Our hope for you is unshaken; for we know that as you share in our sufferings, so also you share in our consolation.

—2 Corinthians 1:3–7

Silence.

...our consolation is abundant through Christ...

Psalm 142 *Voce mea ad Dominum*

1 I cry to the LORD with my voice; *
    to the LORD I make loud supplication.

2 I pour out my complaint before him *
    and tell him all my trouble.

3 When my spirit languishes within me, you know my path; *
    in the way wherein I walk they have hidden a trap for me.

4 I look to my right hand and find no one who knows me; *
    I have no place to flee to, and no one cares for me.

5 I cry out to you, O LORD; *
    I say, "You are my refuge,
    my portion in the land of the living."

6 Listen to my cry for help, for I have been brought very low; *
    save me from those who pursue me,
    for they are too strong for me.

7 Bring me out of prison, that I may give thanks to your Name; *
    when you have dealt bountifully with me,
    the righteous will gather around me.

Prayer

We know, good and gracious God,
    that your will for us is to heal us and make us whole;
yet, Lord, we do not know
    what healing we need;
and we do not always see
    how you can use our weakness
    to draw us closer to each other
            and closer to you,
    how you can use our suffering,
    as you used the suffering of your own Son,
            to redeem us, to renew us,
            and to bring good out of evil.
Use, dear Lord, the prayers we have offered
    to accomplish in us and those we love,
            the good things you alone can give,
                both now and for all eternity. Amen.

THIRD HOUR: God's Care and Healing Power

Prayer

> Lord Jesus Christ,
> > you have made known among us
> > > the healing power of God's love;
> > you gave sight to the blind,
> > > new strength to the lame,
> > > and lifted up those who were sick;
> > you never failed to respond to those
> > > who came to you in faith;
> > help us, then, to turn to you
> > > in that same faith
> > > and to receive from you
> > > the healing you know we need. Amen.

I. JESUS KNOWS OUR NEED

A Reading from the Letter to the Hebrews

It was fitting that God, for whom and through whom all things exist, in bringing many children to glory, should make the pioneer of their salvation perfect through sufferings. For the one who sanctifies and those who are sanctified all have one Father. For this reason Jesus is not ashamed to call them brothers and sisters, saying, "I will proclaim your name to my brothers and sisters, in the midst of the congregation I will praise you." And again, I will put my trust in him." And again, "Here am I and the children whom God has given me." Since, therefore, the children share flesh and blood, he himself likewise shared the same things, so that through death he might destroy the one who has the power of death, that is, the devil, and free those who all their lives were held in slavery by the fear of death. For it is clear that he did not come to help angels, but the descendants of Abraham. Therefore he had to become like his brothers and sisters in every respect, so that he might be a merciful and faithful high priest in the service of God, to make a sacrifice of atonement for the sins of the people. Because he himself was tested by what he suffered, he is able to help those who are being tested. Since, then, we have a great high priest who has passed through the heavens, Jesus, the Son of God, let us hold fast to our confession. For we do not have a high priest who is unable to sympathize with our weaknesses, but we have one who in every respect has been tested as we are, yet without sin. Let us therefore approach the throne of grace with boldness, so that we may receive mercy and find grace to help in time of need.

—Hebrews 2:10–18; 4:14–16

Silence.

...Let us approach the throne of grace with boldness...

Psalm 40:1–8 *Expectans, expectavi*

1 I waited patiently upon the LORD; *
  he stooped to me and heard my cry.

2 He lifted me out of the desolate pit, out of the mire and clay; *
  he set my feet upon a high cliff and made my footing sure.

3 He put a new song in my mouth,
  a song of praise to our God; *
  many shall see, and stand in awe,
  and put their trust in the LORD.

4 Happy are they who trust in the LORD! *
  they do not resort to evil spirits or turn to false gods.

5 Great things are they that you have done, O LORD my God!
  how great your wonders and your plans for us! *
  there is none who can be compared with you.

6 Oh, that I could make them known and tell them! *
  but they are more than I can count.

7 In sacrifice and offering you take no pleasure *
  (you have given me ears to hear you);

8 Burnt-offering and sin-offering you have not required, *
  and so I said, "Behold, I come.

Prayer

You, Lord, have come to us,
  lived among us, and shared our human life;
  you know what it is to be weary, thirsty, and in pain;

you also have overcome even death
and ascended to the right hand of God
to make intercession for us;
we come to you therefore in confidence
that you know our need
and are able to respond
in love and compassion and power.
Hear our prayer, O Lord,
and grant us the gift of perfect trust
that you are doing for us and those we care for
better things than we can either desire or pray for. Amen.

II. GOD'S CARE FOR US

A Reading from the Gospel according to St. Matthew

Jesus said, "Therefore I tell you, do not worry about your life, what you will eat or what you will drink, or about your body, what you will wear. Is not life more than food, and the body more than clothing? Look at the birds of the air; they neither sow nor reap nor gather into barns, and yet your heavenly Father feeds them. Are you not of more value than they? And can any of you by worrying add a single hour to your span of life? And why do you worry about clothing? Consider the lilies of the field, how they grow; they neither toil nor spin, yet I tell you, even Solomon in all his glory was not clothed like one of these. But if God so clothes the grass of the field, which is alive today and tomorrow is thrown into the oven, will he not much more clothe you—you of little faith? Therefore do not worry, saying, 'What will we eat?' or 'What will we drink?' or 'What will we wear?' For it is the Gentiles who strive for all these things; and indeed your heavenly Father knows that you need all these things. But strive first for the kingdom of God and his righteousness, and all these things will be given to you as well. So do not worry about tomorrow, for tomorrow will bring worries of its own. Today's trouble is enough for today."

—Matthew 6:25–34

Silence.

...do not worry about tomorrow...

Psalm 34:1–18 *Benedicam Dominum*

1 I will bless the LORD at all times; *
his praise shall ever be in my mouth.

2 I will glory in the LORD; *
   let the humble hear and rejoice.

3 Proclaim with me the greatness of the LORD;
   let us exalt his Name together.

4 I sought the LORD, and he answered me *
   and delivered me out of all my terror.

5 Look upon him and be radiant, *
   and let not your faces be ashamed.

6 I called in my affliction and the LORD heard me *
   and saved me from all my troubles.

7 The angel of the LORD encompasses those who fear him, *
   and he will deliver them.

8 Taste and see that the LORD is good; *
   happy are they who trust in him!

9 Fear the LORD, you that are his saints, *
   for those who fear him lack nothing.

10 The young lions lack and suffer hunger, *
   but those who seek the LORD lack nothing that is good.

11 Come, children, and listen to me; *
   I will teach you the fear of the LORD.

12 Who among you loves life *
   and desires long life to enjoy prosperity?

13 Keep your tongue from evil-speaking *
   and your lips from lying words.

14 Turn from evil and do good; *
   seek peace and pursue it.

15 The eyes of the LORD are upon the righteous, *
   and his ears are open to their cry.

16 The face of the LORD is against those who do evil, *
    to root out the remembrance of them from the earth.

17 The righteous cry, and the LORD hears them *
    and delivers them from all their troubles.

18 The LORD is near to the brokenhearted *
    and will save those whose spirits are crushed.

Prayer

Most holy and loving God:
    you clothe the grass of the field in glory
        and keep watch over every sparrow;
    yet you came into this world in human flesh
        and have promised to raise
            our mortal bodies to eternal life;
    grant us, then, the gift of faithful trust in your mercy,
        knowing that now and always
            your ears are open to our prayer
        and that you are able to work in all things for our good;
    through Jesus Christ our Lord. Amen.

III. JESUS HEALS THE SICK

A Reading from the Gospel according to St. Mark

They went to Capernaum; and when the sabbath came, he entered the synagogue and taught. They were astounded at his teaching, for he taught them as one having authority, and not as the scribes. Just then there was in their synagogue a man with an unclean spirit, and he cried out, "What have you to do with us, Jesus of Nazareth? Have you come to destroy us? I know who you are, the Holy One of God." But Jesus rebuked him, saying, "Be silent, and come out of him!" And the unclean spirit, convulsing him and crying with a loud voice, came out of him. They were all amazed, and they kept on asking one another, "What is this? A new teaching—with authority! He commands even the unclean spirits, and they obey him." At once his fame began to spread throughout the surrounding region of Galilee. As soon as they left the synagogue, they entered the house of Simon and Andrew, with James and John. Now Simon's mother-in-law was in bed with a fever, and they told him about her at once. He came and took her by the hand and lifted her up. Then the fever left her, and she began to serve them. That evening, at sundown, they brought to him all who were sick or possessed with demons. And the whole city was gathered around the door. And he cured many who were sick with various diseases, and cast out many demons; and he would not permit the demons to speak, because they knew him.

—Mark 1:21–34

Silence.

...he cured many who were sick...

Psalm 138 *Confitebor tibi*

1 I will give thanks to you, O LORD, with my whole heart; *
  before the gods I will sing your praise.

2 I will bow down toward your holy temple
  and praise your Name, *
  because of your love and faithfulness;

3 For you have glorified your Name *
  and your word above all things.

4 When I called, you answered me; *
  you increased my strength within me.

5 All the kings of the earth will praise you, O LORD, *
  when they have heard the words of your mouth.

6 They will sing of the ways of the LORD, *
  that great is the glory of the LORD.

7 Though the LORD be high, he cares for the lowly; *
  he perceives the haughty from afar.

8 Though I walk in the midst of trouble, you keep me safe; *
  you stretch forth your hand against the fury of my enemies;
  your right hand shall save me.

9 The LORD will make good his purpose for me; *
  O LORD, your love endures for ever;
  do not abandon the works of your hands.

Prayer

At evening, Lord Jesus,
   they brought the sick to you,
   and you healed them;
day by day, Lord Jesus,
   you reached out to those who were ill,
      and you healed them;
throughout your ministry on earth, Lord Jesus,
   you never turned away from those who came to you in need,
      but you healed them and gave them new life.
Hear us now, good Lord,
   as we turn to you in our need;
be present with us
   and grant us the gift of healing and wholeness
      that we may rejoice in your love
      and give you glory. Amen.

Silence.

CLOSING PRAYER

Loving and compassionate God,
   you alone are the source of our health and strength;
   you alone enable us to face sickness and danger;
   you alone can provide strength in our weakness;
   you alone hold us up in the hour of our need;
   you alone can give the gift of healing;
   you alone can restore us and make us whole;
hear us, we pray, as we turn to you in love for *N.*
   grant *N.* your strength in *her* weakness;
   grant *her* the knowledge of your presence;
   grant *her* a sure confidence in your mercy;
   and, if it is your will, restore *her*
   to health and strength in your service. Amen.

Silence.

Lord Jesus Christ,
   you came to our world bringing healing;
   you held out your hand to grasp the sick and raise them up;
   you healed the Centurion's son and the Canaanite woman's daughter
      at their request;

you healed the paralyzed man brought to you by his friends;
you healed the woman who touched the hem of your clothing;
so now hear our prayer,
respond to our petitions,
answer us in our time of need,
and let your servant live to give you praise.

Silence.

Holy and life-giving Spirit:
breath of God,
breath of life;
breathe life into your church,
breathe life into all who are sick,
breathe new life and health into *N.*
Renew, revive, inspire, heal, and strengthen your people
with your indwelling power.
Holy and glorious Trinity, one God,
hear our prayer. Amen.

~

a vigil
at the time
of death

~

NOTES FOR
a vigil at the time of death

This form of prayer is designed to be used quietly and meditatively by individuals keeping watch in the church or chapel on the evening before the service for the Burial of the Dead (BCP, pp. 468–505). Those keeping the vigil may use the following materials to help them to focus on God's presence and to hold up the life of the departed in silent offering. Most of the time should be spent in such prayer and meditation.

The vigil material is organized into an opening prayer and three large sections called First Hour, Second Hour, and Third Hour. Each of these hours is composed of four numbered, titled segments. The first three segments in each hour contain a reading and a poetic meditation (psalm, prayer, hymn, or sonnet); the fourth contains a reading and a closing prayer. All participants open with the same opening prayer, then continue their vigil with one of the three hour sections, as assigned. Spend a quarter of an hour on each of the four segments within the hour, contemplating the reading and the psalm and observing silence between them. Silences may also be kept after the psalm, before beginning the next segment. Each participant ends the vigil with the closing prayer that follows the fourth segment in the assigned hour. In this manner, a vigil "hour" may easily last an hour and a half or more. Participants take turns, praying through the three "hour" sections, repeating the cycle for as many hours as desired. Participants who wish to observe longer vigils may ask to be assigned two vigil "hours."

Consider using candles as a way to mark each participant's vigil liturgically. Vigil keepers would light their candles before beginning and leave them burning as others arrive. The final participants end their vigils by extinguishing all candles that have collected over the hours. See notes for A Vigil in the Presence of God for more information.

The Prayer Book provides for a public time of vigil prior to a funeral. The public vigil would then include The Litany at the Time of Death (BCP, pp. 462–464) or Prayers for a Vigil (BCP, pp. 465–466), or both. Following the public vigil, those who wish to do so may continue to keep a vigil through the night by using the readings, psalms, and prayers from the materials provided here as deemed appropriate. If the body is brought into the worship space at the time of the vigil, the prayers for the Reception of the Body would also be used (BCP, pp. 466–467).

a vigil at the time of death

OPENING PRAYER

Eternal and life-giving God:
　　you alone are the source of our life;
　　in you alone we live and move and have our being;
　　through you alone we have the gift of human love and friendship.
All that we have is yours alone,
　　and all that we are and all that we have
　　must return to you at last.
We give you thanks for all your gifts to us:
　　the gifts of love and friendship;
　　the gift of life shared with others;
　　the gift of joy and strength and wisdom received through others;
and, especially, we give you thanks for the life of *N.*,
　　through whose strengths and weaknesses
　　our own lives have been enriched.
Eternal and life-giving God:
help us to entrust *N.*
　　　　　　to your loving and faithful care;
　　help us to return to you in thankfulness
　　the gift of life you gave us in *N.;*
help us to remember that we remain one in Christ,
　　enriched still by your gifts
　　and called still to your service.

FIRST HOUR

I. THE SHORTNESS OF HUMAN LIFE

A Reading from *Holy Dying* by Jeremy Taylor

Since we stay not here, being people but of a day's abode, and our age is like that of a fly and contemporary with a gourd, we must look somewhere else for an abiding city, a place in another country to fix our house in, whose walls and foundation is God, where we must find rest, or else be restless for ever. For whatsoever ease we can have or fancy here is shortly to be changed into sadness or tediousness: it goes away too soon, like the periods of our life: or stays too long, like the sorrows of a sinner: its own weariness, or a contrary disturbance, is its load; or it is eased by its revolution into vanity and forgetfulness; and where there is either sorrow or an end of joy, there can be no true felicity: which because it must be had by some instrument and in some period of our duration, we must carry up our affections to the mansions prepared for us above, where eternity is the measure, felicity is the state, angels are the company, the Lamb is the light, and God is the portion and inheritance.

—Jeremy Taylor, The Rule and Exercises of Holy Dying, *Thomas Wardle, Philadelphia, 1846, pp. 13–14*

Silence.

...we must look elsewhere for an abiding city...

Psalm 103:8–17 *Benedic, anima mea*

8 The LORD is full of compassion and mercy, *
   slow to anger and of great kindness.

9 He will not always accuse us, *
   nor will he keep his anger for ever.

10 He has not dealt with us according to our sins, *
   nor rewarded us according to our wickedness.

11 For as the heavens are high above the earth, *
   so is his mercy great upon those who fear him.

12 As far as the east is from the west, *
   so far has he removed our sins from us.

13 As a father cares for his children, *
   so does the LORD care for those who fear him.

14 For he himself knows whereof we are made; *
   he remembers that we are but dust.

15 Our days are like the grass; *
   we flourish like a flower of the field;

16 When the wind goes over it, it is gone, *
   and its place shall know it no more.

17 But the merciful goodness of the LORD endures for ever
         on those who fear him, *
   and his righteousness on children's children.

II. GOD'S CARE FOR HIS PEOPLE

A Reading from the Prophet Isaiah

Comfort, O comfort my people, says your God. Speak tenderly to Jerusalem, and cry to her that she has served her term, that her penalty is paid, that she has received from the LORD's hand double for all her sins.

A voice cries out: "In the wilderness prepare the way of the LORD, make straight in the desert a highway for our God. Every valley shall be lifted up, and every mountain and hill be made low; the uneven ground shall become level, and the rough places a plain. Then the glory of the LORD shall be revealed, and all people shall see it together, for the mouth of the LORD has spoken."

A voice says, "Cry out!" And I said, "What shall I cry?" All people are grass, their constancy is like the flower of the field. The grass withers, the flower fades, when the breath of the LORD blows upon it; surely the people are grass. The grass withers, the flower fades; but the word of our God will stand forever. Get you up to a high mountain, O Zion, herald of good tidings; lift up your voice with strength, O Jerusalem, herald of good tidings, lift it up, do not fear; say to the cities of Judah, "Here is your God!" See, the Lord GOD comes with might, and his arm rules for him; his reward is with him, and his recompense before him. He will feed his flock like a shepherd; he will gather the lambs in his arms, and carry them in his bosom, and gently lead the mother sheep.

—Isaiah 40:1–11

Silence.

...comfort my people...

Prayer

O God, whose days are without end,
>   and whose mercies cannot be numbered:
Make us, we pray you, deeply sensible
>   of the shortness and uncertainty of life;
and let your Holy Spirit lead us
>   in holiness and righteousness all our days;
that, when we shall have served you in our generation,
>   we may be gathered to our ancestors,
>>   having the testimony of a good conscience;
>   in the communion of the Catholic Church;
>   in the confidence of a certain faith;
>   in the comfort of a reasonable, religious, and holy hope;
>   in favor with you our God;
>   and in perfect charity with the world.
All which we ask through Jesus Christ our Lord. Amen.

—The Book of Common Prayer, p. 489, alt.

III. Preserving the Bonds of Love

A Reading from *Letters and Papers from Prison* by Dietrich Bonhoeffer

Nothing can make up for the absence of someone whom we love, and it would be wrong to try to find a substitute; we must simply hold out and see it through. That sounds very hard at first, but at the same time it is a great consolation, for the gap, as long as it remains unfilled, preserves the bonds between us. It is nonsense to say that God fills the gap; he doesn't fill it, but on the contrary, he keeps it empty and so helps us to keep alive our former communion with each other even at the cost of pain.

Secondly, the dearer and richer our memories, the more difficult the separation. But gratitude changes the pangs of memory into a tranquil joy. The beauties of the past are borne, not as a thorn in the flesh, but as a precious gift in themselves. We must take care not to wallow in our memories or hand ourselves over to them, just as we do not gaze all the time at a valuable present, but only at special times, and apart from these keep it simply as a hidden treasure that is ours for certain. In this way the past gives us lasting joy and strength.

—Dietrich Bonhoeffer, Letters and Papers from Prison,
Eberhard Bethge, ed., Macmillan Publishing Co., 1953, 176–177

Silence.

...the past gives us lasting joy and strength...

Psalm 116:1–5, 10–15 *Dilexi, quoniam*

1 I love the LORD, because he has heard the voice of
    my supplication, *
because he has inclined his ear to me whenever
    I called upon him.

2 The cords of death entangled me;
the grip of the grave took hold of me; *
I came to grief and sorrow.

3 Then I called upon the Name of the LORD: *
"O LORD, I pray you, save my life."

4 Gracious is the LORD and righteous; *
our God is full of compassion.

10 How shall I repay the LORD *
for all the good things he has done for me?

11 I will lift up the cup of salvation *
and call upon the Name of the LORD.

12 I will fulfill my vows to the LORD *
in the presence of all his people.

13 Precious in the sight of the LORD *
is the death of his servants.

14 O LORD, I am your servant; *
I am your servant and the child of your handmaid;
you have freed me from my bonds.

15 I will offer you the sacrifice of thanksgiving *
and call upon the Name of the LORD.

IV. GOING ON ALONE

A Reading from a Letter of John Newton

When my wife died, the world seemed to die with her, (I hope to revive no more.) I see little now, but my ministry and my Christian profession, to make a continuance in life, for a single day, desirable; though I am willing to wait my appointed time. If the world cannot restore her to me, (not that I have the remotest wish that her return was possible,) it can do nothing for me. The Bank of England is too poor to compensate for such a loss as mine. But the Lord, the all-sufficient God, speaks, and it is done. Let those who know him, and trust him, be of good courage. He can give them strength according to their day; he can increase their strength as their trials are increased, to any assignable degree. And what he can do, he has promised he will do. The power and faithfulness on which the successive changes of day and night, and of the seasons of the year, depend, and which uphold the stars in their orbits, is equally engaged to support his people, and to lead them safely and unhurt (if their path be so appointed) through floods and flames. Though I believe she has never yet been (and probably never will be) out of my waking thoughts for five minutes at a time; though I sleep in the bed in which she suffered and languished so long; I have not had one uncomfortable day, nor one restless night, since she left me. I have lost a right hand, which I cannot but miss continually; but the Lord enables me to go on cheerfully without it.

—John Newton, appendix to "Letters to a Wife," in Works *(1824), V, 624–625*

Silence.

...The Lord enables me to go on cheerfully...

Closing Prayer

Gracious and compassionate Lord God,
>you have bound us together with bonds of love
>>in the communion of saints,
>and shown us by raising Jesus from the dead
>that death cannot conquer love
>or divide those who are members of your body.

Grant that we may be so strengthened
>by the knowledge of that unity with those we love
>that we may go on our way
>>with faithfulness and joy in your service. Amen.

SECOND HOUR

I. MARY'S RECOGNITION OF THE RISEN CHRIST

A Reading from the Gospel according to St. John

Mary stood weeping outside the tomb. As she wept, she bent over to look into the tomb; and she saw two angels in white, sitting where the body of Jesus had been lying, one at the head and the other at the feet. They said to her, "Woman, why are you weeping?" She said to them, "They have taken away my Lord, and I do not know where they have laid him." When she had said this, she turned around and saw Jesus standing there, but she did not know that it was Jesus. Jesus said to her, "Woman, why are you weeping? Whom are you looking for?" Supposing him to be the gardener, she said to him, "Sir, if you have carried him away, tell me where you have laid him, and I will take him away." Jesus said to her, "Mary!" She turned and said to him in Hebrew, "Rabbouni!" (which means Teacher). Jesus said to her, "Do not hold on to me, because I have not yet ascended to the Father. But go to my brothers and say to them, 'I am ascending to my Father and your Father, to my God and your God.'" Mary Magdalene went and announced to the disciples, "I have seen the Lord"; and she told them that he had said these things to her.

—John 20:11–18

Silence.

...I have seen the Lord...

Hymn

O what their joy and their glory must be,
those endless Sabbaths the blessed ones see;
crown for the valiant, to weary ones rest:
God shall be all, and in all ever blest.

Truly, "Jerusalem" name we that shore,
city of peace that brings joy evermore;
wish and fulfillment are not severed there,
nor do things prayed for come short of the prayer.

There, where no troubles distraction can bring,
we the sweet anthems of Zion shall sing;
while for thy grace, Lord, their voices of praise
thy blessed people eternally raise.

Now, in the meanwhile, with hearts raised on high,
we for that country must yearn and must sigh,
seeking Jerusalem, dear native land,
through our long exile on Babylon's strand.

Low before him with our praises we fall,
of whom, and in whom, and through whom are all;
of whom, the Father; and in whom, the Son;
through whom, the Spirit, with them ever One.

—Peter Abelard (1079–1142); tr. John Mason Neale (1818–1866),
Hymn #623, The Hymnal 1982, Church Publishing Incorporated

II. RECOGNITION IN RESURRECTION

A Reading from *The Miracles of Our Lord* by George MacDonald

Not to believe in mutual recognition beyond, seems to me a far more reprehensible unbelief than that in the resurrection itself. I can well understand how a man should not believe in any life after death. I will confess that although probabilities are for it, *appearances* are against it. But that a man, still more a woman, should believe in the resurrection of the very same body of Jesus, who took pains that his friends should recognize him therein; that they should regard his resurrection as their one ground for the hope of their own uprising, and yet not believe that friend shall embrace friend in the mansions prepared for them, is to me astounding. Such a shadowy resumption of life I should count unworthy of the name of resurrection. With any theory of the conditions of our resurrection, I have scarcely here to do. It is to me a matter of positively no interest whether or not, in any sense, the matter of our bodies shall be raised from the earth. It is enough that we shall possess forms capable of revealing ourselves and of bringing us into contact with God's other works; forms in which the idea, so blurred and broken in these, shall be carried out—remaining so like that friends shall doubt not a moment of the identity, becoming so unlike, that the tears of recognition shall be all for the joy of the gain and the gratitude of the loss.

—George MacDonald, The Miracles of Our Lord

Silence.

...friend shall embrace friend...

Prayer

> Almighty God,
>> we entrust all who are dear to us
>>> in this life and the life to come,
>>> to your never-failing love,
>> knowing that you are doing for them
>>> better things than we can desire or pray for;
>> through Jesus Christ our Lord. Amen.

> —The Book of Common Prayer, *p. 831, alt.*

III. THE JOURNEY OF HUMAN LIFE

A Reading from *The Crown of the Year* by Austin Farrer

Our journey sets out from God in our creation, and returns to God at the final judgement. As the bird rises from the earth to fly, and must some time return to the earth from which it rose; so God sends us forth to fly, and we must fall back into the hands of God at last. But God does not wait for the failure of our power and the expiry of our days to drop us back into his lap. He goes himself to meet us and everywhere confronts us. Where is the countenance which we must finally look in the eyes and not be able to turn away our head? It smiles up at Mary from the cradle, it calls Peter from the nets, it looks on him with grief when he has denied his master. Our judge meets us at every step of our way, with forgiveness on his lips and succour in his hands. He offers us these things while there is yet time. Every day opportunity shortens, our scope for learning our Redeemer's love is narrowed by twenty-four hours, and we come nearer to the end of our journey, when we shall fall into the hands of the living God, and touch the heart of the devouring fire.

> —*Austin Farrer,* The Crown of the Year,
> *Dacre Press, Westminster, 1952, pp. 7–8, 10*

Silence.

...we must fall back into God's hands...

Psalm 139:1–17, 22–23 *Domine, probasti*

> 1 LORD, you have searched me out and known me; *
>> you know my sitting down and my rising up;
>> you discern my thoughts from afar.

> 2 You trace my journeys and my resting-places *
>> and are acquainted with all my ways.

3 Indeed, there is not a word on my lips, *
but you, O LORD, know it altogether.

4 You press upon me behind and before *
and lay your hand upon me.

5 Such knowledge is too wonderful for me; *
it is so high that I cannot attain to it.

6 Where can I go then from your Spirit? *
where can I flee from your presence?

7 If I climb up to heaven, you are there; *
if I make the grave my bed, you are there also.

8 If I take the wings of the morning *
and dwell in the uttermost parts of the sea,

9 Even there your hand will lead me *
and your right hand hold me fast.

10 If I say, "Surely the darkness will cover me, *
and the light around me turn to night,"

11 Darkness is not dark to you;
the night is as bright as the day; *
darkness and light to you are both alike.

12 For you yourself created my inmost parts; *
you knit me together in my mother's womb.

13 I will thank you because I am marvelously made; *
your works are wonderful, and I know it well.

14 My body was not hidden from you, *
while I was being made in secret
and woven in the depths of the earth.

15 Your eyes beheld my limbs, yet unfinished in the womb;
all of them were written in your book; *
they were fashioned day by day,
when as yet there was none of them.

16 How deep I find your thoughts, O God! *
      how great is the sum of them!

17 If I were to count them, they would be more in number
                    than the sand; *
      to count them all, my life span would need to
                    be like yours.

22 Search me out, O God, and know my heart; *
      try me and know my restless thoughts.

23 Look well whether there be any wickedness in me *
      and lead me in the way that is everlasting.

IV. FAITH GIVES US ASSURANCE

A Reading from the Letter to the Hebrews

Now faith is the assurance of things hoped for, the conviction of things not seen. Indeed, by faith our ancestors received approval. By faith we understand that the worlds were prepared by the word of God, so that what is seen was made from things that are not visible.

By faith Abraham obeyed when he was called to set out for a place that he was to receive as an inheritance; and he set out, not knowing where he was going. By faith he stayed for a time in the land he had been promised, as in a foreign land, living in tents, as did Isaac and Jacob, who were heirs with him of the same promise. For he looked forward to the city that has foundations, whose architect and builder is God.

All of these died in faith without having received the promises, but from a distance they saw and greeted them. They confessed that they were strangers and foreigners on the earth, for people who speak in this way make it clear that they are seeking a homeland. If they had been thinking of the land that they had left behind, they would have had opportunity to return. But as it is, they desire a better country, that is, a heavenly one. Therefore God is not ashamed to be called their God; indeed, he has prepared a city for them.

And what more should I say? For time would fail me to tell of Gideon, Barak, Samson, Jephthah, of David and Samuel and the prophets—who through faith conquered kingdoms, administered justice, obtained promises, shut the mouths of lions, quenched raging fire, escaped the edge of the sword, won strength out of weakness, became mighty in war, put foreign armies to flight.

Women received their dead by resurrection. Others were tortured, refusing to accept release, in order to obtain a better resurrection. Others suffered mocking and flogging, and even chains and imprisonment. They were stoned to death, they were sawn in two, they were killed by the sword; they went about in skins of sheep and goats, destitute, persecuted, tormented—of whom the world was not worthy. They wandered in deserts and mountains, and in caves and holes in the ground.

Yet all these, though they were commended for their faith, did not receive what was promised, since God had provided something better so that they would not, apart from us, be made perfect.

Therefore, since we are surrounded by so great a cloud of witnesses, let us also lay aside every weight and the sin that clings so closely, and let us run with perseverance the race that is set before us, looking to Jesus the pioneer and perfecter of our faith, who for the sake of the joy that was set before him endured the cross, disregarding its shame, and has taken his seat at the right hand of the throne of God.

—Hebrews 11:1–3, 8–10, 13–16, 32–40; 12:1–2

Silence.

...so great a cloud of witnesses...

Closing Prayer

Bring us, O Lord God, at our last awakening
   into the house and gate of heaven,
to enter into that gate and dwell in that house,
   where there shall be no darkness nor dazzling,
      but one equal light;
   no noise nor silence,
      but one equal music;
   no fears nor hopes,
      but one equal possession;
   no ends nor beginnings,
      but one equal eternity;
in the habitations of thy glory and dominion
   world without end. Amen.

—John Donne

THIRD HOUR

I. The Destined Journey

A Reading from *The Hymn of the Universe* by Teilhard de Chardin

Death will not simply throw us back into the great flux of reality, as the pantheist's picture of beatitude would have us believe. Nevertheless in death we are caught up, overwhelmed, dominated by that divine power which lies within the forces of inner disintegration and, above all, within that irresistible yearning which will drive the separated soul on to complete its further, predestined journey as infallibly as the sun causes the mists to rise from the water on which it shines. Death surrenders us completely to God; it makes us pass into God. In return we have to surrender ourselves to it, in love and in the abandon of love, since, when death comes to us, there is nothing further for us to do but let ourselves be entirely dominated and led onwards by God.

> —*Teilhard de Chardin*, The Hymn of the Universe,
> *Simon Bartholomew, trans., Harper and Row, 1961, p. 150*

Silence.

...Death surrenders us to God...

A Sonnet

Death be not proud, though some have called thee
Mighty and dreadfull, for, thou art not soe,
For, those, whom thou think'st, thou dost overthrow,
Die not, poore death, nor yet canst thou kill mee.
From rest and sleepe, which but thy pictures bee,
Much pleasure, then from thee, much more must flow,
And soonest our best men with thee doe goe,
Rest of their bones, and soules deliverie.
Thou art slave to Fate, Chance, kings, and desperate men,
And dost with poyson, warre, and sicknesse dwell,
And poppie, or charmes can make us sleepe as well,
And better then thy stroake; why swell'st thou then?
One short sleepe past, wee wake eternally,
And death shall be no more; death, thou shalt die.

> —*John Donne*

II. THE PROMISE OF LIFE

A Reading from the Gospel according to St. John

Martha said to Jesus, "Lord, if you had been here, my brother would not have died. But even now I know that God will give you whatever you ask of him." Jesus said to her, "Your brother will rise again." Martha said to him, "I know that he will rise again in the resurrection on the last day." Jesus said to her, "I am the resurrection and the life. Those who believe in me, even though they die, will live, and everyone who lives and believes in me will never die."

—John 11:21–26

Silence.

...Those who believe in me will live...

Prayer

You, O Lord, are Resurrection,
    and you, O Lord, are Life.
Grant us so to believe your promise
    that we and all those who belong to you
        may come with joy to the resurrection life
    that you have promised us
        and opened to us
    through your death and resurrection. Amen.

III. THE BLESSEDNESS OF HEAVEN

A Reading from a Sermon by John Donne

I would ask permission of the angels of heaven, of the Holy Spirit also, to say a little of the everlasting blessedness of the kingdom of heaven. The tongues of angels cannot, the tongues of the Holy Spirit, the authors of the books of scripture, have not told us what this blessedness is. What then shall we say except this? Blessedness itself is God. Our blessedness is our possession, our union with God. Of what does this consist? Many great teachers place this blessedness, this union with God, in this: that in heaven I shall see God, see God face to face. We do not see anyone in that way in this world. In this world we see only outsides; in heaven I shall see God, and God's essence.

But many other teachers place this blessedness, this union with God, in love: that in heaven I shall love God. Now love presumes knowledge, for we can only love what we understand or think we understand. There in heaven I shall know God which means I shall be admitted not only to an adoration of God, a reverence of God, but to more familiarity with God, more equality with God, so that I may love God. But even love itself, as noble a passion as it is, is only a pain unless we enjoy what we love. Therefore still other teachers place this blessedness, this union of our souls with God, in our joy, our enjoyment of God. In this world we enjoy nothing. Enjoyment requires continuance, and here all things are fluid and transitory. There I shall enjoy and possess forever God as God is. But every one of these, to see God, or to love God, or to enjoy God, has seemed to some too narrow to fully include this blessedness beyond which nothing can be imagined. Therefore other teachers place this blessedness in all these together. And truly, if any of these did exclude any others so that I might see God and not love God or love God without enjoyment, it could not well be called blessedness; but those who have any one of these have every one and all.

In heaven therefore I shall have not only vision, not only a seeing, but a beholding, a contemplating of God. I shall have an uninterrupted sight of God. I shall look, and never look away; not look, and look again, as here, but look, and look still.

I shall see the whole light. Here I see some parts of the air enlightened by the sun, but I do not see the whole light of the sun. There I shall see God entirely, all God, I myself shall be all light to see that light by. Here I have one faculty enlightened and another left in darkness; my understanding sometimes clear, my will at the same time perverted. There I shall be all light, no shadow upon me; my soul invested in the light of joy and my body in the light of glory.

—*George R. Potter and Evelyn M. Simpson,* The Sermons of John Donne, *University of California Press, Vol. 9, pp. 127–129*

Silence.

...*I shall see God...*

A Hymn of Christ's Triumph over Death

> Crown him with many crowns, the Lamb upon his throne;
> Hark! how the heavenly anthem drowns all music but its own;
> awake, my soul, and sing of him who died for thee,
> and hail him as thy matchless King through all eternity.
>
> Crown him the Lord of life, who triumphed o'er the grave,
> and rose victorious in the strife for those he came to save;
> his glories now we sing who died, and rose on high,
> who died, eternal life to bring, and lives that death may die.

—*Matthew Bridges,*
Hymn #494, stanzas 1,3, The Hymnal 1982,
Church Publishing Incorporated

IV. THE VISION OF HEAVEN

A Reading from the Book of Revelation

Then I saw a new heaven and a new earth; for the first heaven and the first earth had passed away, and the sea was no more. And I saw the holy city, the new Jerusalem, coming down out of heaven from God, prepared as a bride adorned for her husband. And I heard a loud voice from the throne saying,

"See, the home of God is among mortals.

He will dwell with them;

they will be his peoples,

and God himself will be with them;

he will wipe every tear from their eyes.

Death will be no more;

mourning and crying and pain will be no more,

for the first things have passed away."

And the one who was seated on the throne said, "See, I am making all things new." Also he said, "Write this, for these words are trustworthy and true." Then he said to me, "It is done! I am the Alpha and the Omega, the beginning and the end. To the thirsty I will give water as a gift from the spring of the water of life. Those who conquer will inherit these things, and I will be their God and they will be my children.

—Revelation 21:1–7

Silence.

...God will be with them...

Closing Prayer

Faithful and life-giving God:

we thank you for all those

who served you in ages past

and left us an example of faithfulness;

we thank you for *N.*,

who served you in this life

and has now entered eternal life

to live forever with you

and with all those who have gone before us;

help us, we pray, to follow in faith

where Jesus has led the way

and many others have followed,

so that we, with them, may win the eternal victory

which you have promised;

through the same Jesus Christ our Lord. Amen.

a vigil for maundy thursday

NOTES FOR

a vigil for maundy thursday

The Maundy Thursday vigil developed over the years as a natural expression of reverence toward the bread and wine by means of which, according to Jesus' promise, he continues to come to us. The vigil is usually kept after the Maundy Thursday evening service at a chapel or side altar where some of the bread and, depending on local practice, also sometimes the wine that were consecrated during the Maundy Thursday Eucharist have been reserved for use on Good Friday (a day on which the Eucharist is not celebrated). Church members wishing to keep this vigil sign up to spend an hour or two in prayer at this altar, taking turns in order to keep an uninterrupted watch over the bread and wine in which Christ is present. The vigil may continue through the night until the beginning of the Good Friday liturgy.

There are two very different, even contradictory, themes expressed in this vigil. One is the theme of hope, thankfulness, even awe, as keepers of the vigil sit or kneel for long periods meditating upon the gift of the Body and Blood of Christ. The first bestowal of this gift by Christ to his disciples is, of course, conveyed particularly and powerfully during the Maundy Thursday liturgy itself and will still be fresh upon participants' minds. The other theme is somber, even to the point of despair, and is established at the very end of the Maundy Thursday liturgy when the altar is stripped bare and the people leave in silence without benefit of the usual final blessing or dismissal. Such starkness is in marked contrast to the reassuring and nurturing mood which predominates in the liturgy. This abrupt change in tone naturally and inevitably leads the keepers of the vigil to realize that they are taking part in the Maundy Thursday vigil in order to accomplish that which Jesus asked his disciples to do on the first Maundy Thursday vigil two thousand years ago: to be with him in prayerful preparation for his death on Good Friday. "Could you not watch with me one hour?" he asked when he discovered them all sleeping.

The materials provided here reflect both these themes. It is suggested that those keeping this vigil move back and forth between themes as much as they find comfortable and appropriate; those who prefer to focus only on one theme also should feel free to do so. More material has been provided than will be needed. Do not try to use it all, but rather select material that will help you to use the silence most profitably and nourish your sense of Christ's presence.

The material that follows is divided into eight segments consisting of a reading, psalm or hymn, and prayer. There is also an opening prayer and a closing prayer which each participant may use at the beginning and end of his or her vigil time. It is suggested that participants spend at least fifteen minutes with each segment and move through not more than four segments in an hour. Those organizing the vigil might let participants use the various segments as they choose, or ask participants to use the first four segments in the first hour and the second four segments in the second hour, so alternating through the time of the vigil.

The Maundy Thursday vigil kept in this traditional way may seem like a simple matter for a few members of a community to undertake, but it is not. Preparation for—and education about—the vigil must begin during Lent with service bulletin notices, posters, and sign-up sheets. This vigil presents unusual problems and challenges. For example, participants will be coming and going at odd hours of the night, and in some neighborhoods, their arrivals and departures may raise safety concerns. The place of vigil should be secure yet accessible; entrances should be conspicuous and well lit. There should be at least two—and preferably three—persons in (or near) the place of vigil at any time. A cell phone, portable phone, or standard phone should be easily available to them in case of need.

a vigil for
maunoy thursoay

OPENING PRAYER

Let all human flesh be silent
and stand with fear and trembling
and think of nothing earthly, nothing unholy;
the king of kings and Lord of Lords,
Christ our God comes to us
and gives himself as food for his people.
All the glorious companies of angels
behold this and wonder
and love and worship Jesus.
Every throne and dominion,
the cherubim with sleepless eyes
and the seraphim with many wings,
cover their faces before the majesty of his glory
and sing a perpetual hymn of praise. Amen.

—Liturgy of St. James, para. Jeremy Taylor,
Selected Works, *Thomas K. Carroll, ed.,*
Paulist Press, 1990, p. 214

I. WATCHING WITH CHRIST

A Reading from the Gospel according to St. Matthew

Then Jesus went with them to a place called Gethsemane; and he said to his disciples, "Sit here while I go over there and pray." He took with him Peter and the two sons of Zebedee, and began to be grieved and agitated. Then he said to them, "I am deeply grieved, even to death; remain here, and stay awake with me." And going a little farther, he threw himself on the ground and prayed, "My Father, if it is possible, let this cup pass from me; yet not what I want but what you want." Then he

101

came to the disciples and found them sleeping; and he said to Peter, "So, could you not stay awake with me one hour? Stay awake and pray that you may not come into the time of trial; the spirit indeed is willing, but the flesh is weak." Again he went away for the second time and prayed, "My Father, if this cannot pass unless I drink it, your will be done." Again he came and found them sleeping, for their eyes were heavy. So leaving them again, he went away and prayed for the third time, saying the same words. Then he came to the disciples and said to them, "Are you still sleeping and taking your rest? See, the hour is at hand, and the Son of Man is betrayed into the hands of sinners. Get up, let us be going. See, my betrayer is at hand."

—Matthew 26:36–46

Silence.

...*stay awake with me*...

Psalm 62:1–2, 6–9 *Nonne Deo?*

1 For God alone my soul in silence waits; *
from him comes my salvation.

2 He alone is my rock and my salvation, *
my stronghold, so that I shall not be greatly shaken.

6 For God alone my soul in silence waits; *
truly, my hope is in him.

7 He alone is my rock and my salvation, *
my stronghold, so that I shall not be shaken.

8 In God is my safety and my honor; *
God is my strong rock and my refuge.

9 Put your trust in him always, O people, *
pour out your hearts before him, for God is our refuge.

Prayer

Lord Jesus,
you have called us to watch with you
as you called your disciples to watch on this night;
you have asked us to pray with you
that our Father's will may be done
though it may not be our will;

help us, Lord, to let go of our own will
and to seek our Father's will more fully;
help us to wait with you and watch with you
and to use times of waiting
to watch and pray
and be present with you
hour by hour and day by day
so that others may know presence with us
and be drawn to you;
Grant, Lord, that you may find us awake and watchful
this night and always. Amen.

II. THE FEAST OF LOVE

A Reading from the Book of Deuteronomy

Remember the long way that the LORD your God has led you these forty years in the wilderness, in order to humble you, testing you to know what was in your heart, whether or not you would keep his commandments. He humbled you by letting you hunger, then by feeding you with manna, with which neither you nor your ancestors were acquainted, in order to make you understand that one does not live by bread alone, but by every word that comes from the mouth of the LORD.

—Deuteronomy 8:2–3

Silence.

...not by bread alone...

Psalm 78:1–4, 12–25 *Attendite, popule*

1 Hear my teaching, O my people; *
incline your ears to the words of my mouth.

2 I will open my mouth in a parable; *
I will declare the mysteries of ancient times.

3 That which we have heard and known,
and what our forefathers have told us, *
we will not hide from their children.

4 We will recount to generations to come
the praiseworthy deeds and the power of the LORD, *
and the wonderful works he has done.

12 He worked marvels in the sight of their forefathers, *
   in the land of Egypt, in the field of Zoan.

13 He split open the sea and let them pass through; *
   he made the waters stand up like walls.

14 He led them with a cloud by day, *
   and all the night through with a glow of fire.

15 He split the hard rocks in the wilderness *
   and gave them drink as from the great deep.

16 He brought streams out of the cliff, *
   and the waters gushed out like rivers.

17 But they went on sinning against him, *
   rebelling in the desert against the Most High.

18 They tested God in their hearts, *
   demanding food for their craving.

19 They railed against God and said, *
   "Can God set a table in the wilderness?

20 True, he struck the rock, the waters gushed out, and the
                  gullies overflowed; *
   but is he able to give bread
   or to provide meat for his people?"

21 When the LORD heard this, he was full of wrath; *
   a fire was kindled against Jacob,
   and his anger mounted against Israel;

22 For they had no faith in God, *
   nor did they put their trust in his saving power.

23 So he commanded the clouds above *
   and opened the doors of heaven.

24 He rained down manna upon them to eat *
   and gave them grain from heaven.

25 So mortals ate the bread of angels; *
he provided for them food enough.

Prayer

From the beginning, gracious and loving God,
you have provided food for your people:

you fed us with manna in the wilderness,
and, though we strayed from you and wandered for many years,
you led us finally into a land flowing with milk and honey;

you sent us a Savior
who fed multitudes in the desert
and offered his own body and blood
to his disciples;

as you have always fed us, feed us still, good and gracious God;
nourish us with your presence at your table
and, in the silence of this vigil,
this night and always. Amen.

III. The Lord Will Prepare a Feast

A Reading from the Prophet Isaiah

On this mountain the LORD of hosts will make for all peoples a feast of rich food, a feast of well-aged wines, of rich food filled with marrow, of well-aged wines strained clear. And he will destroy on this mountain the shroud that is cast over all peoples, the sheet that is spread over all nations; he will swallow up death forever. Then the Lord GOD will wipe away the tears from all faces, and the disgrace of his people he will take away from all the earth, for the LORD has spoken. It will be said on that day, Lo, this is our God; we have waited for him, so that he might save us. This is the LORD for whom we have waited; let us be glad and rejoice in his salvation.

—*Isaiah 25:6–9*

Silence.

...a feast for all peoples...

Psalm 34:1–10 *Benedicam Dominum*

1 I will bless the LORD at all times; *
his praise shall ever be in my mouth.

2 I will glory in the LORD; *
let the humble hear and rejoice.

3 Proclaim with me the greatness of the LORD; *
let us exalt his Name together.

4 I sought the LORD, and he answered me *
and delivered me out of all my terror.

5 Look upon him and be radiant, *
and let not your faces be ashamed.

6 I called in my affliction and the LORD heard me *
and saved me from all my troubles.

7 The angel of the LORD encompasses those who fear him, *
and he will deliver them.

8 Taste and see that the LORD is good; *
happy are they who trust in him!

9 Fear the LORD, you that are his saints, *
for those who fear him lack nothing.

10 The young lions lack and suffer hunger, *
but those who seek the LORD lack nothing that is good.

Prayer

We wait for you, Lord God;
day by day we seek you
and find you present in all of life;
you greet us in the rising sun,
in the warmth of family and friends,
in the needs of those who are sick or hungry,
troubled or dying;

you come to us when we pray,
    when we study your written word,
    and in the bread and wine of the altar;
grant that others may find you present in the life of your people
    and rejoice in your salvation. Amen.

IV. The Marriage Feast in Heaven

A Reading from the Book of Revelation

After this I heard what seemed to be the loud voice of a great multitude in heaven, saying, "Hallelujah! Salvation and glory and power to our God, for his judgments are true and just.... And the twenty-four elders and the four living creatures fell down and worshiped God who is seated on the throne, saying, "Amen. Hallelujah!" And from the throne came a voice saying, "Praise our God, all you his servants, and all who fear him, small and great." Then I heard what seemed to be the voice of a great multitude, like the sound of many waters and like the sound of mighty thunder peals, crying out, "Hallelujah! For the Lord our God the Almighty reigns. Let us rejoice and exult and give him the glory, for the marriage of the Lamb has come, and his bride has made herself ready; to her it has been granted to be clothed with fine linen, bright and pure"—for the fine linen is the righteous deeds of the saints. And the angel said to me, "Write this: Blessed are those who are invited to the marriage supper of the Lamb." And he said to me, "These are true words of God."

—*Revelation 19:1–2a, 4–9*

Silence.

...the marriage supper of the Lamb...

A Hymn

O food of souls wayfaring,
The bread of angels sharing,
    O manna from on high
We hunger; Lord, supply us,
Nor your delights deny us
    Whose hearts to you draw nigh.

O stream of love past telling,
O purest fountain welling
    Out from the Savior's side!

107

We faint with thirst; revive us,
Of your abundance give us,
   All that we need provide.

O Jesus, by you bidden,
We here adore you, hidden
   In gifts of bread and wine;
Grant, when the veil is riven,
We may behold in heaven
   Your countenance divine.

—from the Maintzisch Gesangbuch, 1661

Prayer

O God, in a wonderful sacrament you have left us a perpetual memorial of the death and resurrection of your Son, Jesus Christ our Lord; grant us so to venerate the mystery of his presence that we may always see within ourselves the fruit of his redeeming love; through the same, your Son, Jesus Christ our Lord. Amen.

—Thomas Aquinas

V. THIS IS CHRIST'S BODY

A Reading from *The Crown of the Year* by Austin Farrer

This is my body, said Christ at the Supper, and it was so. He is well able to consecrate bread, for he speaks the word of God. The world itself only exists because God said that it should be so, and it was so. Christ has consecrated bread, and it is consecrated; his consecration takes effect upon our altars. But why should he consecrate bread? Only that the consecration of the bread might extend, and embrace the company which partakes of the bread. "This is my body," he declares, and it is his body. We receive it, and we are his body, signed, sealed, consecrated by the word which made the world.

—Austin Farrer, The Crown of the Year,
Dacre Press, Westminster, 1952, p. 38

Silence.

...we are his body...

A Hymn

Humbly I adore thee, Verity unseen,
Who thy glory hidest, 'neath these shadows mean;
Lo, to thee surrendered, my whole heart is bowed
Tranced as it beholds thee, shrined within the cloud.

Taste and touch and vision to discern thee fail;
Faith that comes by hearing pierces through the veil.
I believe whate'er the Son of God hath told;
What the Truth hath spoken, that for truth I hold.
On the Cross lay hidden but thy Deity,
Here, too, is concealed thy humanity
But in both believing and confessing, Lord,
Ask I what the dying thief of thee implored.

Thy dread wounds, like Thomas, though I cannot see,
His be my confession, Lord and God, of thee.
Lord, my faith unfeigned evermore increase;
Give me hope unfailing, love that cannot cease.

O Memorial wondrous of the Lord's own death,
Living bread that givest all thy creatures breath
Grant my spirit ever by thy life may live,
To my taste thy sweetness never failing give.

Jesus, whom now veiled, I by faith descry,
What my soul doth thirst for, do not, Lord, deny,
That thy face unveiled I at last may see,
With the blissful vision blest, my God, of thee.

—Thomas Aquinas

Prayer

O Lord,
I am not worthy or fit
that you should come under the roof
    of the house of my soul
because it is wholly desolate and ruinous;
nor do you have in me a fitting place
    to lay your head.

But as you were willing
  to lie in a cave and manger with the animals,
as you did not disdain
  to enter even the house of Simon the leper,
as you did not reject
  the harlot, a sinner like me,
  coming to you and touching you,
  nor yet the thief upon the cross;
even so, permit me also,
  a sinner beyond measure,
  to touch, receive, and partake of
  the most pure, excellent, life-giving
  and saving mysteries
  of your most holy Body
  and your most precious Blood.
And grant us communion,
  faith that need not be ashamed,
  love without dissimulation,
  fulfillment of your commandments,
  stirring up every spiritual gift,
  turning away all adversity,
  healing of soul and body,
  symbol of our gathering together;
that we also, with all your saints
who have been pleasing to you from the beginning,
  may be partakers of your eternal gifts
which you, Lord, have prepared for those who love you,
  and in whom you are glorified for ever. Amen.

—*Lancelot Andrewes, alt.*

Silence.

VI. OBEYING CHRIST'S COMMAND

A Reading from *The Shape of the Liturgy* by Dom Gregory Dix

At the heart of it all is the eucharistic action, a thing of an absolute simplicity—the taking, blessing, breaking and giving of bread and the taking, blessing and giving of a cup of wine and water, as these were first done with their new
meaning by a young Jew before and after supper with His friends on the night
before He died. He had told his friends to do this henceforward with the new
meaning for the anamnesis of Him, and they have done it always since.

Was ever another command so obeyed? For century after century, spreading slowly to every continent and country and among every race on earth, this action has been done, in every conceivable human circumstance, for every conceivable human need from infancy and before it to extreme old age and after it, from the pinnacles of earthly greatness to the refuge of fugitives in the caves and dens of the earth. Men have found no better thing than this to do for kings at their crowning and for criminals going to the scaffold; for armies in triumph or for a bride and bridegroom in a little country church; for the proclamation of a dogma or for a good crop of wheat; for the wisdom of the Parliament of a mighty nation or for a sick old woman afraid to die; for a schoolboy sitting an examination or for Columbus setting out to discover America; for the famine of whole provinces or for the soul of a dead lover; in thankfulness because my father did not die of pneumonia; for a village headman much tempted to return to fetich because the yams had failed; because the Turk was at the gates of Vienna; for the repentance of Margaret; for the settlement of a strike; for a son for a barren woman; for Captain so-and-so, wounded and prisoner of war; while the lions roared in the nearby amphitheatre; on the beach at Dunkirk; while the hiss of scythes in the thick June grass came faintly through the windows of the church; tremulously, by an old monk on the fiftieth anniversary of his vows; furtively, by an exiled bishop who had hewn timber all day in a prison camp near Murmansk; gorgeously, for the canonisation of S. Joan of Arc—one could fill many pages with the reasons why men have done this, and not tell a hundredth part of them. And best of all, week by week and month by month, on a hundred thousand successive Sundays, faithfully, unfailingly, across all the parishes of christendom, the pastors have done this just to make the *plebs sancta Dei*—the holy common people of God.

—*Dom Gregory Dix,* The Shape of the Liturgy,
Dacre Press, London, 1945, p. 744

Silence.

...*Was ever another command so obeyed?*...

Psalm 43 *Judica me, Deus*

1 Give judgment for me, O God,
  and defend my cause against an ungodly people; *
  deliver me from the deceitful and the wicked.

2 For you are the God of my strength;
  why have you put me from you? *
  and why do I go so heavily while the enemy
    oppresses me?

3 Send out your light and your truth, that they may lead me, *
   and bring me to your holy hill
   and to your dwelling;

4 That I may go to the altar of God,
   to the God of my joy and gladness; *
   and on the harp I will give thanks to you, O God my God.

5 Why are you so full of heaviness, O my soul? *
   and why are you so disquieted within me?

6 Put your trust in God; *
   for I will yet give thanks to him,
   who is the help of my countenance, and my God.

Prayer

You call us, Lord Jesus, to share the feast
which you first shared with the disciples
on the night before your death upon the cross;
the same life you shared with them
   is shared with us;
the same love you poured forth on the cross
is poured forth in this feast;
this is the feast which your saints share for ever
and to which we also are called;
this is the feast of our forgiveness, redemption, health, and joy;
let us come then to this table and share this feast;
and as we come to you, Lord Jesus,
come now and always to us. Amen.

—*Eric Milner-White,* My God My Glory
SPCK, London, 1954, p. 82, alt.

VII. THE CENTER OF THE UNIVERSE

A Reading from *The Hymn of the Universe* by Teilhard de Chardin

Lord God, when I go up to your altar for communion, grant that I may derive from it a discernment of the infinite perspectives hidden beneath the smallness and closeness of the host in which you are concealed. Already I have accustomed myself to recognize beneath the inertness of the morsel of bread a consuming power which, as the greatest Doctors of your Church have said, far from being absorbed into me, absorbs me into itself. Help me now to overcome that remaining illusion which would make me think of you as touching me only in a limited and momentary way. I begin to understand: under the sacramental species you touch me first of all through the "accidents" of matter, of the material bread; but then, in consequence of this, you touch me also through the entire universe inasmuch as the entire universe, thanks to that primary influence, ebbs and flows over me. In a true sense the arms and the heart which you open to me are nothing less than all the united powers of the world which, permeated through and through by your will, your inclinations, your temperament, bend over my being to form it and feed it and draw it into the blazing centre of your infinite fire. In the host, Lord Jesus, you offer me myself.

—*Teilhard de Chardin*, The Hymn of the Universe,
Harper & Row, New York, p. 76

Silence.

...you touch me also through the entire universe...

Psalm 145:1–10, 14–22 *Exaltabo te, Deus*

1 I will exalt you, O God my King, *
and bless your Name for ever and ever.

2 Every day will I bless you *
and praise your Name for ever and ever.

3 Great is the LORD and greatly to be praised; *
there is no end to his greatness.

4 One generation shall praise your works to another *
and shall declare your power.

5 I will ponder the glorious splendor of your majesty *
and all your marvelous works.

6 They shall speak of the might of your wondrous acts, *
and I will tell of your greatness.

7 They shall publish the remembrance of your great goodness; *
they shall sing of your righteous deeds.

8 The LORD is gracious and full of compassion, *
slow to anger and of great kindness.

9 The LORD is loving to everyone *
   and his compassion is over all his works.

10 All your works praise you, O LORD, *
   and your faithful servants bless you.

14 The LORD is faithful in all his words *
   and merciful in all his deeds.

15 The LORD upholds all those who fall; *
   he lifts up those who are bowed down.

16 The eyes of all wait upon you, O LORD, *
   and you give them their food in due season.

17 You open wide your hand *
   and satisfy the needs of every living creature.

18 The LORD is righteous in all his ways *
   and loving in all his works.

19 The LORD is near to those who call upon him, *
   to all who call upon him faithfully.

20 He fulfills the desire of those who fear him; *
   he hears their cry and helps them.

22 My mouth shall speak the praise of the LORD; *
   let all flesh bless his holy Name for ever and ever.

Prayer

Father, we thank you for planting your church in our hearts
   and imparting life to us through your Son Jesus Christ.
As grain was planted on the hillsides
   and made into the one loaf
   which is broken on our altars,
so may we at last be gathered into one church
   to the glory of your great Name. Amen.

—inspired by a passage from The Didache

VIII. The Living Bread

A Reading from the Gospel according to St. John

Jesus said, "Very truly, I tell you, whoever believes has eternal life. I am the bread of life. Your ancestors ate the manna in the wilderness, and they died. This is the bread that comes down from heaven, so that one may eat of it and not die. I am the living bread that came down from heaven. Whoever eats of this bread will live forever; and the bread that I will give for the life of the world is my flesh."

The Jews then disputed among themselves, saying, "How can this man give us his flesh to eat?" So Jesus said to them, "Very truly, I tell you, unless you eat the flesh of the Son of Man and drink his blood, you have no life in you. Those who eat my flesh and drink my blood have eternal life, and I will raise them up on the last day; for my flesh is true food and my blood is true drink. Those who eat my flesh and drink my blood abide in me, and I in them. Just as the living Father sent me, and I live because of the Father, so whoever eats me will live because of me. This is the bread that came down from heaven, not like that which your ancestors ate, and they died. But the one who eats this bread will live forever."

—John 6:47–58

Silence.

...I am the bread of life...

Psalm 34:1–5, 7–8 *Benedicam Dominum*

1 I will bless the LORD at all times; *
   his praise shall ever be in my mouth.

2 I will glory in the LORD; *
   let the humble hear and rejoice.

3 Proclaim with me the greatness of the LORD; *
   let us exalt his Name together.

4 I sought the LORD, and he answered me *
   and delivered me out of all my terror.

5 Look upon him and be radiant, *
   and let not your faces be ashamed.

7 The angel of the LORD encompasses those who fear him, *
   and he will deliver them.

8 Taste and see that the LORD is good; *
   happy are they who trust in him!

Prayer

   Bread of heaven, life of the world,
      raise us up, we pray, to the throne of your glory,
         that we may know the power of your loving presence
            and may go out from this place
            to make that loving presence known to others;
   let the gifts of love, of unity, and of peace
    be found always in us
        and through us in all the world. Amen

CLOSING PRAYER

An act of praise for the presence of Christ in the sacrament

   Blessed be God.
   Blessed be God's holy Name.
   Blessed be Jesus Christ, truly God, truly human.
   Blessed be the Holy Spirit, the Strengthener.
   Blessed be the Mother of God, Mary most holy.
   Blessed be God in the angels and in the saints.
   Blessed, praised, and adored be Jesus Christ
    on his throne of glory in heaven,
    in the holy sacrament of the altar,
    and in the hearts of his people,
   Blessed be God. Amen.

~

the vigil
of
pentecost

~

NOTES FOR
the vigil of pentecost

Pentecost, the festival of the Holy Spirit, ranks traditionally just after Easter in importance in the church's calendar. An indication of its importance in the early church was that Pentecost was the most likely occasion—after Easter—for Baptisms. A vigil of Pentecost serves two very special purposes: spiritually, it affords an opportunity to meditate upon the gifts of the Holy Spirit in an intentional and specific way; liturgically, it offers today's congregation an opportunity to restore to Pentecost some of the prominence assumed by other festivals, such as Christmas, over the last few centuries.

The proper liturgical ranking of Pentecost may not at first seem especially significant—certainly not as significant as our need to acknowledge the gifts of the Spirit—until one remembers that there is intention and design in the Christian calendar; that its yearly unfolding generates nothing less than a complete and perpetually repeated course of Christian education; that even the juxtaposition of seasons and festivals has instructional intent. Among the lessons the church calendar teaches every year is that the Day of Pentecost—which follows the Easter season in seasonal rotation as well as in importance—is a culmination of the months of Lenten preparation and Paschal celebration. The Pentecost story of the apostles gathered together to receive the outpouring of the Holy Sprit represents the completed prototype of what the church should be—a people empowered by the Spirit's presence.

The progression of the calendar through Lent, Holy Week, Easter, and eventually Pentecost teaches us, then, to look forward to the church's mission while, at the same time, reminding us of the journey we have already made. Pentecost, a Greek word meaning "the fiftieth day" was originally the Greek name sometimes used for the Jewish Feast of Weeks, which fell on the fiftieth day after Passover. Passover was the Jewish festival Jesus celebrated with his disciples on the night before he was crucified. A modern congregation that holds a Great Vigil of Easter on the Saturday night before Easter Day and then holds another vigil seven weeks later on the evening before Pentecost is reenacting a rhythm of worship many thousands of years old. This pairing of these prominent evening observances—which in some sense "kick off" the celebration of the two central holy days—will recall Christian worshipers to the Jewish manner of religious observance (i.e., always beginning at sundown) and will strengthen in their minds the already strong historical ties between Passover/Jewish Pentecost and Easter/Christian Pentecost.

The Vigil of Pentecost that follows was written specifically to draw upon and build upon the rich legacy of early church practices—practices which will place the congregation at the very crossroads of our ongoing Christian faith and our ancient spiritual heritage. The Prayer Book rubrics (BCP, pp. 175, 227) describe a simple Vigil of Pentecost based on the Service of Light (BCP, pp. 109–112). The rubrics say that the church should be "dark, or partially so" and that the "Paschal Candle, if used, should be burning in its customary place before the people assemble." The Prayer Book does not specify a late evening service— the most popular time for Easter Vigils—but nighttime has the backing of tradition, and an evening setting contributes greatly to the reverential drama of the occasion. In a parish that ordinarily celebrates a Eucharist early on Saturday evening, it may be appropriate to keep the vigil beforehand; otherwise, it is preferable to keep the vigil later that night, in keeping with Easter Vigil practice; a "sunrise" vigil is another possibility, although it would be best to begin before daylight so that the Paschal Candle burning alone inside the dimly lit church will make a strong welcoming impression upon arriving worshipers.

The service described in the Prayer Book begins with the Service of Light and uses the Paschal Candle to light the smaller candles on or near the altar. The approach described here, however, provides a form of the Service of Light that is integral, rather than prefatory, to the vigil. Seven candles—preferably placed in a line or half-circle behind the altar—are lit one at a time throughout the vigil, following the lesson for each of the seven segments provided here. These candles represent the seven gifts of the spirit (as discerned by Christian tradition and drawn from the Vulgate translation of a passage from Isaiah): wisdom, understanding, counsel, fortitude, knowledge, piety, and fear of the Lord. If a shorter service requiring fewer than seven segments is planned, all seven candles should still be lit, but more than one might be lit following some of the canticles. A seven-branched menorah, as contrasted to the better known nine-branch Hanukkah candlestick (which more properly is called a "hanukiah") might well be used instead of separate candle stands. The menorah—in Jewish worship symbolizing the seven days of creation—will serve as a powerful additional link to our spiritual heritage.

The opening hymn, "Come, Holy Ghost, our souls inspire," (*The Hymnal 1982,* #503 or #504) may be sung antiphonally by cantor and congregation or in unison, either in procession or after the ministers are in place. Note that metrical versions of two of the canticles (see First and Second Canticles of the Spirit) are provided in an "Alternate Metrical Canticles" section following the vigil. Following the practice of the Easter Vigil, the lessons should be announced by segment title ("The Giving of the Law at Mount Sinai") rather than by the usual Bible source citation ("A Reading from the Book of Exodus"). If the Eucharist is celebrated, the Peace and the Offertory may follow immediately after the last lesson (John 7:37–39a) given here. For all the reasons of tradition and association explained above, the Eucharist forms the most appropriate completion of this

119

service, especially if that is the local liturgical practice for the Great Vigil of Easter. Alternatively, the full order for the Eucharist may follow Baptism or Renewal of Baptismal Vows.

the vigil of pentecost

Introit Hymn: *Come, Holy Ghost, our souls inspire*

—The Hymnal 1982, #503 or #504

A deacon or other minister then says or sings the following:

Rejoice now, Holy Church, with all creation,
  for God has sent the Holy Spirit into our hearts
  to call us out of darkness into light;
on this day the Holy Spirit, who moved over the waters
  in the darkness of eternal night before the Creation,
  comes with fire to illuminate our darkness;
on this day the Holy Spirit, who spoke through the prophets
  to condemn injustice and give hope to the oppressed,
  comes with fire to purge our world;
on this day the Holy Spirit, who descended upon Jesus
  to proclaim him God's anointed one,
  comes with fire to reveal God's love;
on this day the Holy Spirit, who came upon the apostles at Pentecost
  to send them out into all the world
  and to proclaim the gospel to all people,
  comes with fire to renew and inspire the Church;
on this day we gather as the Church, the people of God,
  to renew our baptismal commitment
  and to be renewed by the Spirit's gifts,
  that we may bear witness to the power of God
  for the healing and uniting of all people,
  to the glory and praise of our Creator, Redeemer,
      and Sanctifier. *Amen.*

Let us now hear from Holy Scripture and other witnesses of the work of the Holy Spirit in ages past, and let us pray that the same Spirit will guide and inspire the church in our day, both in this community and throughout the world.

THE GIVING OF THE LAW AT MOUNT SINAI

On the third new moon after the Israelites had gone out of the land of Egypt, on that very day, they came into the wilderness of Sinai. They had journeyed from Rephidim, entered the wilderness of Sinai, and camped in the wilderness; Israel camped there in front of the mountain. Then Moses went up to God; the LORD called to him from the mountain, saying, "Thus you shall say to the house of Jacob, and tell the Israelites: You have seen what I did to the Egyptians, and how I bore you on eagles' wings and brought you to myself. Now therefore, if you obey my voice and keep my covenant, you shall be my treasured possession out of all the peoples. Indeed, the whole earth is mine, but you shall be for me a priestly kingdom and a holy nation. These are the words that you shall speak to the Israelites."

So Moses came, summoned the elders of the people, and set before them all these words that the LORD had commanded him. The people all answered as one: "Everything that the LORD has spoken we will do." Moses reported the words of the people to the LORD. Then the LORD said to Moses, "I am going to come to you in a dense cloud, in order that the people may hear when I speak with you and so trust you ever after...."

On the morning of the third day there was thunder and lightning, as well as a thick cloud on the mountain, and a blast of a trumpet so loud that all the people who were in the camp trembled. Moses brought the people out of the camp to meet God. They took their stand at the foot of the mountain. Now Mount Sinai was wrapped in smoke, because the LORD had descended upon it in fire; the smoke went up like the smoke of a kiln, while the whole mountain shook violently. As the blast of the trumpet grew louder and louder, Moses would speak and God would answer him in thunder. When the LORD descended upon Mount Sinai, to the top of the mountain, the LORD summoned Moses to the top of the mountain, and Moses went up....

When all the people witnessed the thunder and lightning, the sound of the trumpet, and the mountain smoking, they were afraid and trembled and stood at a distance, and said to Moses, "You speak to us, and we will listen; but do not let God speak to us, or we will die." Moses said to the people, "Do not be afraid; for God has come only to test you and to put the fear of him upon you so that you do not sin."

—Exodus 19:1–9, 16–20; 20:18–20

Silence.

In the silence following the reading of the lesson, a flame is carried from the Paschal Candle to light one of the seven candles, representing the first day of creation and one of the seven gifts of the Spirit: Fear of the Lord.

Psalm 33:12–22 *Exultate, justi*

12 Happy is the nation whose God is the LORD! *
happy the people he has chosen to be his own!

13 The LORD looks down from heaven, *
and beholds all the people in the world.

14 From where he sits enthroned he turns his gaze *
on all who dwell on the earth.

15 He fashions all the hearts of them *
and understands all their works.

16 There is no king that can be saved by a mighty army;
a strong man is not delivered by his great strength.

17 The horse is a vain hope for deliverance; *
for all its strength it cannot save.

18 Behold, the eye of the LORD is upon those who fear him, *
on those who wait upon his love,

19 To pluck their lives from death, *
and to feed them in time of famine.

20 Our soul waits for the Lord; *
he is our help and our shield.

21 Indeed, our heart rejoices in him, *
for in his holy Name we put our trust.

22 Let your loving-kindness, O LORD, be upon us, *
as we have put our trust in you.

Let us pray.

Eternal God, who spoke to Moses and called your people into covenant through the giving of the Law, speak to us, we pray, and renew us in your covenant that we may be your holy people, now and always. *Amen.*

GOD PROMISES TO RENEW THE COVENANT
BY SENDING THE SPIRIT INTO HUMAN HEARTS

Thus says the Lord GOD: It is not for your sake, O house of Israel, that I am about to act, but for the sake of my holy name, which you have profaned among the nations to which you came. I will sanctify my great name, which has been profaned among the nations, and which you have profaned among them; and the nations shall know that I am the LORD, says the Lord GOD, when through you I display my holiness before their eyes. I will take you from the nations, and gather you from all the countries, and bring you into your own land. I will sprinkle clean water upon you, and you shall be clean from all your uncleannesses, and from all your idols I will cleanse you. A new heart I will give you, and a new spirit I will put within you; and I will remove from your body the heart of stone and give you a heart of flesh. I will put my spirit within you, and make you follow my statutes and be careful to observe my ordinances. Then you shall live in the land that I gave to your ancestors; and you shall be my people, and I will be your God.

—Ezekiel 36:22–28

Silence.

During the silence, a flame is carried from the Paschal Candle to light one of the seven candles, representing the second day of creation and another of the seven gifts of the Spirit: Counsel.

Psalm 105:1–11, 39–45 *Confitemini Domino*

1 Give thanks to the LORD and call upon his Name; *
   make known his deeds among the peoples.

2 Sing to him, sing praises to him, *
   and speak of all his marvelous works.

3 Glory in his holy Name; *
   let the hearts of those who seek the LORD rejoice.

4 Search for the LORD and his strength; *
   continually seek his face.

5 Remember the marvels he has done, *
   his wonders and the judgments of his mouth,

6 O offspring of Abraham his servant, *
   O children of Jacob his chosen.

7 He is the LORD our God; *
  his judgments prevail in all the world.

8 He has always been mindful of his covenant, *
  the promise he made for a thousand generations:

9 The covenant he made with Abraham, *
  the oath that he swore to Isaac,

10 Which he established as a statute for Jacob, *
   an everlasting covenant for Israel,

11 Saying, "To you will I give the land of Canaan *
   to be your allotted inheritance."

39 He spread out a cloud for a covering *
   and a fire to give light in the night season.

40 They asked, and quails appeared, *
   and he satisfied them with bread from heaven.

41 He opened the rock, and water flowed, *
   so the river ran in the dry places.

42 For God remembered his holy word *
   and Abraham his servant.

43 So he led forth his people with gladness, *
   his chosen with shouts of joy.

44 He gave his people the lands of the nations, *
   and they took the fruit of others' toil,

45 That they might keep his statutes *
   and observe his laws.
   Hallelujah!
 Let us pray.

God of unchanging purpose and everlasting mercy: cleanse and renew our hearts by the indwelling power of your Holy Spirit, that we may be your people and make known your holiness in all the world; through Jesus Christ our Lord. *Amen.*

THE VARIED GIFTS OF THE SPIRIT ARE DESCRIBED

Wisdom, the fashioner of all things, taught me. There is in her a spirit that is intelligent, holy, unique, manifold, subtle, mobile, clear, unpolluted, distinct, invulnerable, loving the good, keen, irresistible, beneficent, humane, steadfast, sure, free from anxiety, all-powerful, overseeing all, and penetrating through all spirits that are intelligent, pure, and altogether subtle. For wisdom is more mobile than any motion; because of her pureness she pervades and penetrates all things. For she is a breath of the power of God, and a pure emanation of the glory of the Almighty; therefore nothing defiled gains entrance into her. For she is a reflection of eternal light, a spotless mirror of the working of God, and an image of his goodness Although she is but one, she can do all things, and while remaining in herself, she renews all things; in every generation she passes into holy souls and makes them friends of God, and prophets; for God loves nothing so much as the person who lives with wisdom. She is more beautiful than the sun, and excels every constellation of the stars. Compared with the light she is found to be superior, for it is succeeded by the night, but against wisdom evil does not prevail. She reaches mightily from one end of the earth to the other, and she orders all things well.

—The Wisdom of Solomon 7:22–30; 8:1

Silence.

During the silence, a flame is carried from the Paschal Candle to light one of the seven candles, representing the third day of creation and another of the seven gifts of the Spirit: Wisdom.

Psalm 104:25–37 *Benedic, anima mea*

25 O LORD, how manifold are your works! *
    in wisdom you have made them all;
    the earth is full of your creatures.

26 Yonder is the great and wide sea
    with its living things too many to number, *
    creatures both small and great.

27 There move the ships,
    and there is that Leviathan, *
    which you have made for the sport of it.

28 All of them look to you *
    to give them their food in due season.

29 You give it to them; they gather it; *
    you open your hand, and they are filled with good things.

30 You hide your face, and they are terrified; *
   you take away their breath,
   and they die and return to their dust.

31 You send forth your Spirit, and they are created; *
   and so you renew the face of the earth.

32 May the glory of the LORD endure for ever; *
   may the LORD rejoice in all his works.

33 He looks at the earth and it trembles; *
   he touches the mountains and they smoke.

34 I will sing to the LORD as long as I live; *
   I will praise my God while I have my being.

35 May these words of mine please him; *
   I will rejoice in the LORD.

36 Let sinners be consumed out of the earth, *
   and the wicked be no more.

37 Bless the LORD, O my soul. *
   Hallelujah!

Let us pray.

Breathe in us, Almighty God, so that your holy and life-giving Spirit, reflection of your light and renewer of all created things, may fill your Church and order all things to your glory, by the power of that same Spirit; through Christ our Lord. *Amen.*

THE SPIRIT TEACHES AND ENABLES OUR PRAYER

All who are led by the Spirit of God are children of God. For you did not receive a spirit of slavery to fall back into fear, but you have received a spirit of adoption. When we cry, "Abba! Father!" it is that very Spirit bearing witness with our spirit that we are children of God, and if children, then heirs, heirs of God and joint heirs with Christ—if, in fact, we suffer with him so that we may also be glorified with him.

I consider that the sufferings of this present time are not worth comparing with the glory about to be revealed to us. For the creation waits with eager longing for the revealing of the children of God.... We know that the whole creation has been groaning in labor pains until now; and not only the creation, but we ourselves, who have the first fruits of the Spirit, groan inwardly while we wait for adoption, the redemption of our bodies. For in hope we were saved. Now hope that is seen is not hope. For who hopes for what is seen? But if we hope for what we do not see, we wait for it with patience.

Likewise the Spirit helps us in our weakness; for we do not know how to pray as we ought, but that very Spirit intercedes with sighs too deep for words. And God, who searches the heart, knows what is the mind of the Spirit, because the Spirit intercedes for the saints according to the will of God.

—Romans 8:14–19; 22–27

Silence.

During the silence, a flame is carried from the Paschal Candle to light one of the seven candles, representing the fourth day of creation and another of the seven gifts of the Spirit: Knowledge.

The following may be sung or recited in unison or antiphonally.

The First Canticle of the Spirit

Now there are varieties of gifts, but the same Spirit;
and there are varieties of services, but the same Lord;
and there are varieties of activities,
but it is the same God who activates all of them in everyone.
To each is given the manifestation of the Spirit for the common good.
To one is given through the Spirit the utterance of wisdom,
to another the utterance of knowledge according to the same Spirit,
to another faith by the same Spirit,
to another gifts of healing by the one Spirit,
to another the working of miracles,
to another prophecy,
to another the discernment of spirits,
to another various kinds of tongues,
to another the interpretation of tongues.
All these are activated by one and the same Spirit,
who allots to each one individually just as the Spirit chooses.
For in the one Spirit we were all baptized into one body—
Jews or Greeks, slaves or free—
and we were all made to drink of one Spirit.

—1 Corinthians 12:4–11, 13

Let us pray.

Holy Spirit, you teach us to pray to the Father with sighs too deep for words: open our hearts to your indwelling presence so we may grow in that abundant life promised us by our Lord and Savior Jesus Christ. *Amen.*

THE GROWTH OF THE SPIRIT IN US IS DESCRIBED

Pentecost is not the feast of the Holy Ghost, it is the feast of his descent upon us. The Son of God came down and was made man in the womb of Mary. The Holy Ghost came down and was made human in the souls of Christians. When Jesus was ripe for birth, he left Mary's womb, to grow up and be himself. He outgrew first her womb and then her lap, first her protection, last her person and her mind. But as the Holy Ghost grows in us, it is not he but we who grow. He does not grow up and leave us behind, we grow up into him. He becomes the spring and substance of our mind and heart. He is the never failing fountain of which Jesus spoke to the Samaritan woman. We break up the stony rubble of our life again and again, to find and release the well of living water.

—*Austin Farrer,* The Crown of the Year
Dacre Press, Westminister, 1952, p. 36

Silence.

During the silence, a flame is carried from the Paschal Candle to light one of the seven candles, representing the fifth day of creation and another of the seven gifts of the Spirit: Understanding.

Canticle 12: Invocation, Part III, and Doxology

Glorify the Lord, all you works of the Lord, *
      praise him and highly exalt him for ever.
In the firmament of his power, glorify the Lord, *
      praise him and highly exalt him for ever.

Let the people of God glorify the Lord, *
      praise him and highly exalt him for ever.
Glorify the Lord, O priests and servants of the Lord, *
      praise him and highly exalt him for ever.

Glorify the Lord, O spirits and souls of the righteous, *
      praise him and highly exalt him for ever.
You that are holy and humble of heart, glorify the Lord, *
      praise him and highly exalt him for ever.

Let us glorify the Lord: Father, Son, and Holy Spirit; *
　　　praise him and highly exalt him for ever.
In the firmament of his power, glorify the Lord, *
　　　praise him and highly exalt him for ever.

—The Book of Common Prayer, pp. 88–90

Let us pray.

Well-spring of life, let your Holy Spirit grow in us to refresh and renew your people, that we may bring life to all the world in your holy Name. *Amen.*

THE DEMANDS OF THE HOLY SPIRIT ON US ARE DESCRIBED

When we pray "Come, Holy Ghost, our souls inspire," we had better know what we are about. He will not carry us to easy triumphs and gratifying successes; more probably he will set us to some task for God in the full intention that we shall fail, so that others, learning wisdom by our failure, may carry the good cause forward. He may take us through loneliness, desertion by friends, apparent desertion even by God; that was the way Christ went to the Father. He may drive us into the wilderness to be tempted of the devil. He may lead us from the Mount of Transfiguration (if he ever lets us climb it) to the hill that is called the Place of a Skull. For if we invoke him, it must be to help us in doing God's will not ours. We cannot call upon the

　　　Creator Spirit, by whose aid
　　　The world's foundations first were laid

in order to use omnipotence for the supply of our futile pleasures or the success of our futile plans. If we invoke him, we must be ready for the glorious pain of being caught by his power out of our petty orbit into the eternal purposes of the Almighty, in whose onward sweep our lives are but a speck of dust. The soul that is filled with the Spirit must have become purged of all pride or love of ease, all self-complacence and self-reliance; but that soul has found the only real dignity, the only lasting joy. Come, then, Great Spirit, come. Convict the world and convict my timid soul.

—William Temple, Readings in St. John's Gospel,
MacMillan and Co. Ltd., London, 1950, pp. 288–289

Silence.

During the silence, a flame is carried from the Paschal Candle to light one of the seven candles, representing the sixth day of creation and another of the seven gifts of the Spirit: Fortitude.

Psalm 139:1–13, 16, 22–23 *Domine, probasti*

1 LORD, you have searched me out and known me; *
　　　you know my sitting down and my rising up;
　　　you discern my thoughts from afar.

2 You trace my journeys and my resting-places *
   and are acquainted with all my ways.

3 Indeed, there is not a word on my lips, *
   but you, O LORD, know it altogether.

4 You press upon me behind and before *
   and lay your hand upon me.

5 Such knowledge is too wonderful for me; *
   it is so high that I cannot attain to it.

6 Where can I go then from your Spirit? *
   where can I flee from your presence?

7 If I climb up to heaven, you are there; *
   if I make the grave my bed, you are there also.

8 If I take the wings of the morning *
   and dwell in the uttermost parts of the sea,

9 Even there your hand will lead me *
   and your right hand hold me fast.

10 If I say, "Surely the darkness will cover me, *
   and the light around me turn to night,"

11 Darkness is not dark to you;
   the night is as bright as the day; *
   darkness and light to you are both alike.

12 For you yourself created my inmost parts; *
   you knit me together in my mother's womb.

13 I will thank you because I am marvelously made; *
   your works are wonderful, and I know it well.

16 How deep I find your thoughts, O God! *
   how great is the sum of them!

22 Search me out, O God, and know my heart; *
   try me and know my restless thoughts.

23 Look well whether there be any wickedness in me *
   and lead me in the way that is everlasting.

Let us pray.

O God of unchangeable power and eternal light: Look favorably upon your whole Church, that wonderful and sacred mystery; by the effectual working of your providence, carry out in tranquility the plan of salvation; let the whole world see and know that things which were cast down are being raised up, and things which had grown old are being made new, and that all things are being brought to their perfection by him through whom all things were made, your Son Jesus Christ our Lord. *Amen.*

—The Book of Common Prayer, pp. 280, 528

JESUS PROMISES THE HOLY SPIRIT TO THOSE WHO BELIEVE IN HIM

On the last day of the festival, the great day, while Jesus was standing there, he cried out, "Let anyone who is thirsty come to me, and let the one who believes in me drink. As the scripture has said, 'Out of the believer's heart shall flow rivers of living water.'" Now he said this about the Spirit, which believers in him were to receive.

—John 7:37–39a

Silence.

During the silence, a flame is carried from the Paschal Candle to light the last of the seven candles, representing the seventh day of creation and the last of the seven gifts of the Spirit: Piety.

The Second Canticle of the Spirit

Blessed are those who wash their robes,
   so that they will have the right to the tree of life
   and may enter the city by the gates.
The Spirit and the bride say, "Come."
And let everyone who hears say, "Come."
And let everyone who is thirsty come.
Let anyone who wishes take the water of life as a gift.

—Revelation 22:14, 17

Let us pray.

O God, you created all things by the power of your Word, and you renew the earth by your Spirit: Give now the water of life to those who thirst for you, that they may bring forth abundant fruit in your glorious kingdom; through Jesus Christ our Lord. *Amen.*

—The Book of Common Prayer, p. 290

Holy Baptism (beginning with the Presentation of the Candidates, and concluding with the reception of the newly baptized) may be administered here or, if the Eucharist is celebrated, after the Gospel. Confirmation may also be administered.

In the absence of candidates for Baptism or Confirmation, the Celebrant leads the people in the Renewal of Baptismal Vows, either here or, if the Eucharist is celebrated, after the Gospel.

The bishop or priest first addresses the congregation in these or similar words:

Through the gift of the Holy Spirit, dear friends, we are given renewal of life and strengthened for witness in the world. I call upon you, therefore, in this season of the Spirit to renew the solemn promises and vows of Holy Baptism in which we were sealed with that same Holy Spirit and marked as Christ's own for ever. *Amen.*

The Renewal of Baptismal Vows

Book of Common Prayer (pages 292–294)

The Holy Eucharist

Book of Common Prayer (pages 361–366 or alternative eucharistic prayers)

alternate metrical canticles

The First Canticle of the Sprit

1 Corinthians 12:4–11, 13

1 The gifts of God are given us
    In great diversity,
    But in them all the Spirit works
    Creating unity.

2 We serve our God in many ways
    Yet all that we have done
    Has been empowered by one God
    At work in everyone.

3 To build community, God's gifts
    Are manifest in each:
    The gift of knowledge or the gift
    Of wisdom in our speech.

4 To some the gift of healing comes,
    To others prophecy,
    Discernment, miracles, and tongues,
    But all for unity.

5 For just as we were baptized in
    One Spirit, so are we
    Made one in Christ, both Jews and Greeks,
    And whether slave or free.

The Second Canticle of the Spirit

1 The Spirit and the bride
    Are speaking and say, "Come";
    Let everyone who hears these words
    Respond now and say, "Come."

2 The one who testifies
    Says, "Surely I will come";
    Let all respond to this and say,
    "Amen. Lord Jesus, come."

~

a vigil before
the election
or ordination
of a bishop

~

*(which may also be used before the selection or ordination
of deacons and priests, or the selection of other church leaders,
or the celebration of any new ministry)*

a Vigil Before the election or ordination of a Bishop

This vigil was designed primarily as a private vigil to be kept by a small number of individuals by turns over a period of many hours in the cathedral (or perhaps at several locations around the diocese) before the election or ordination of a bishop. There are several possible adaptations of the model: as a private vigil kept before the selection or ordination of a deacon or priest; as a private vigil celebration before the beginning of a new ministry; as a private vigil before the calling of a parish or diocesan lay professional (such as an administrator, a Christian educator, or a director of music) or the election of wardens and vestry; as a public vigil kept on any of these occasions.

For a private vigil

Print out enough copies of the materials supplied here, or materials modeled on them, for all participants, and have them waiting—along with instructions— for those who will keep the vigil. There are six numbered segments (not counting the opening and closing prayers). Participants should spend at least twenty minutes with each segment. A participant who goes through all six plus the opening and closing prayers should spend slightly more than two hours in prayer and meditation. If the vigil is to last many hours, participants may simply go back over the entire vigil again and again by turns. If shorter stints are preferred, ask participants to pray the opening prayer, then the first three segments or, by turns, the last three, followed by the closing prayer.

You may wish to mark the cumulative progress of the vigil by lighting candles (see instructions for a private vigil in the notes for A Vigil in the Presence of God).

Review the additional instructions in the introduction to this book.

For a public vigil

Leaders and readers direct the congregation in the prayers, in saying the psalms, and in keeping the silences. The themes or "titles" for each numbered segment can be announced by the leader and/or projected overhead at the appropriate moment (see notes for A Vigil in the Presence of God for additional details, and also see the instructions in the introduction to this book).

For the first of the two opening prayers ("Opening Prayer for God's

Presence") consider praying responsively, with the congregation reading the italicized psalmic insertions.

For a public or private vigil for a deacon, priest, or lay minister

To adapt this vigil to the appointment or ordination of a deacon or priest, the appointment of a lay minister, or the celebration of any new ministry, see the Alternate Readings section which immediately follows this vigil. Most of the necessary adaptations need to be made in the fifth segment ("Mutual Ministry"). Instead of the readings supplied there, insert the appropriate alternate readings (or similar readings of your own choosing). In a few other places throughout the vigil, the word "bishop" (or some other term) appears in italics—following established Prayer Book style—to signal that other words may be inserted as necessary.

Additional variations

Most of the readings, psalms, and prayers provided in the earlier vigil, A Vigil in the Presence of God, may be used to begin this vigil when it is being kept as a long watch through the night.

a vigil before the election or ordination of a bishop

OPENING PRAYERS

Prayer for God's Presence

Lord God, you have built your Church
on the foundation of the apostles and prophets,
and you sent your Holy Spirit to guide and empower your church
    for the work of ministry;
it is through that guidance alone
that we can make right choices
    to carry on the work of ministry;
you alone know the thoughts of human hearts;
you alone can enable us to discern the gifts you have given.
Help us now to open ourselves to the presence of your Spirit;
be with us in the quiet and peace of this time of prayer and listening;
make us instruments of your will for your Church,
that we may choose a *bishop*
    prepared to serve your people and glorify your Name.
You are great, O God, and worthy of highest praise;
you stir in us the joy of praising you,
since you have made us for yourself,
and our hearts are restless
until they find rest in you.

One thing have I asked of the LORD; one thing I seek;
    that I may dwell in the house of the LORD all the days of my life;
To behold the fair beauty of the LORD
    and to seek him in his temple.
For God alone my soul in silence waits;
    from him comes my salvation.

                        —Psalms 27:5–6, 62:1

God of peace,
let us rest in your presence;
let us keep watch in your holy place;
let our restless thoughts be stilled;
let your peace sink deep into our souls;
let your presence be sufficient for us
as we keep watch before you.

I wait for the LORD; my soul waits for him;
in his word is my hope.
O Israel, wait for the LORD,
for with the LORD there is mercy.

—Psalm 130:4, 6

Let your mercy, O Lord, be with those who keep watch this night
    with those who seek for peace in human hearts;
    with those who preach the gospel
        to those who have not heard it;
    with those who witness to the gospel
        to those who have not seen it;
    with those who work for healing tonight
        in places of conflict,
        in hospitals and homes;
with those who bring your presence
        to those who need your love and healing power.

Be present, Lord Christ, with those who watch this night:
    with those who are ill;
    with those who are dying;
    with those who are hungry;
    with those who are homeless;
    with those who rejoice
        in the birth of a child,
        in a marriage,
        in an anniversary,
        in prayers answered,
        in the gift of love,
        in the confidence of faith;
    with those who wait for the Spirit's gift.

Grant that our waiting and watching this night
may draw us closer to your love. Amen.

Prayer for Guidance

> Lord, it is through the guidance of your Spirit alone
> that we make right judgments
> and come to know your will
> for ourselves and for your church;
> help us to seek that guidance
> and to find it and to follow it,
> so that your people may know your will
> and make known your love. Amen.

I. The Vision of God's Holiness and Calling

A Reading from the Prophet Isaiah

In the year that King Uzziah died, I saw the Lord sitting on a throne, high and lofty; and the hem of his robe filled the temple. Seraphs were in attendance above him; each had six wings: with two they covered their faces, and with two they covered their feet, and with two they flew. And one called to another and said: "Holy, holy, holy is the LORD of hosts; the whole earth is full of his glory." The pivots on the thresholds shook at the voices of those who called, and the house filled with smoke. And I said: "Woe is me! I am lost, for I am a man of unclean lips, and I live among a people of unclean lips; yet my eyes have seen the King, the LORD of hosts!"

Then one of the seraphs flew to me, holding a live coal that had been taken from the altar with a pair of tongs. The seraph touched my mouth with it and said: "Now that this has touched your lips, your guilt has departed and your sin is blotted out." Then I heard the voice of the Lord saying, "Whom shall I send, and who will go for us?" And I said, "Here am I; send me!"

—Isaiah 6:1–8

Silence.

...Whom shall I send?...

Psalm 99 *Dominus regnavit*

> 1 The LORD is King;
>   let the people tremble; *
>   he is enthroned upon the cherubim;
>   let the earth shake.

2 The LORD is great in Zion; *
   he is high above all peoples.

3 Let them confess his Name, which is great and awesome; *
   he is the Holy One.

4 "O mighty King, lover of justice, you have established equity; *
   you have executed justice and righteousness in Jacob."

5 Proclaim the greatness of the LORD our God
   and fall down before his footstool; *
   he is the Holy One.

6 Moses and Aaron among his priests,
   and Samuel among those who call upon his Name, *
   they called upon the LORD, and he answered them.

7 He spoke to them out of the pillar of cloud; *
   they kept his testimonies and the decree that he gave them.

8 O LORD our God, you answered them indeed; *
   you were a God who forgave them,
   yet punished them for their evil deeds.

9 Proclaim the greatness of the LORD our God
   and worship him upon his holy hill; *
   for the LORD our God is the Holy One.

Prayer

Most holy God, enthroned in glory above the seraphim;
   you call us to bear witness to your glory
         and proclaim the glory of your Name;
   help us, we pray, in our various ministries,
         to make known the glory you have shown us
   so that all people may be drawn to worship you;
         through Jesus Christ our Lord. Amen.

II. Jesus Calls Us as Friends and Promises the Spirit's Guidance

A Reading from the Gospel according to St. John

Jesus said, "This is my commandment, that you love one another as I have loved you. No one has greater love than this, to lay down one's life for one's friends. You are my friends if you do what I command you. I do not call you servants any longer, because the servant does not know what the master is doing; but I have called you friends, because I have made known to you everything that I have heard from my Father. You did not choose me but I chose you. And I appointed you to go and bear fruit, fruit that will last, so that the Father will give you whatever you ask him in my name. I am giving you these commands so that you may love one another.

"If the world hates you, be aware that it hated me before it hated you. If you belonged to the world, the world would love you as its own. Because you do not belong to the world, but I have chosen you out of the world—therefore the world hates you. Remember the word that I said to you, 'Servants are not greater than their master.' If they persecuted me, they will persecute you; if they kept my word, they will keep yours also. But they will do all these things to you on account of my name, because they do not know him who sent me. If I had not come and spoken to them, they would not have sin; but now they have no excuse for their sin. Whoever hates me hates my Father also. If I had not done among them the works that no one else did, they would not have sin. But now they have seen and hated both me and my Father. It was to fulfill the word that is written in their law, 'They hated me without a cause.'

"When the Advocate comes, whom I will send to you from the Father, the Spirit of truth who comes from the Father, he will testify on my behalf. You also are to testify because you have been with me from the beginning."

—John 15:12–27

Silence.

...You did not choose me but I chose you...

Psalm 51:11–16 *Miserere mei, Deus*

11 Create in me a clean heart, O God, *
and renew a right spirit within me.

12 Cast me not away from your presence *
and take not your holy Spirit from me.

13 Give me the joy of your saving help again *
    and sustain me with your bountiful Spirit.

14 I shall teach your ways to the wicked, *
    and sinners shall return to you.

15 Deliver me from death, O God, *
    and my tongue shall sing of your righteousness,
    O God of my salvation.

16 Open my lips, O Lord, *
    and my mouth shall proclaim your praise.

Prayer

Guide your church, everliving God,
    by the power and presence of your Holy Spirit,
        so that we will answer when we are called,
            and seek the gifts we need for service,
            and serve you where we are sent;
    to the honor and glory of your Name. Amen.

III. ALL MINISTRY IS BUILT ON CHRIST

A Reading from the First Letter to the Corinthians

According to the grace of God given to me, like a skilled master builder I laid a foundation, and someone else is building on it. Each builder must choose with care how to build on it. For no one can lay any foundation other than the one that has been laid; that foundation is Jesus Christ. Now if anyone builds on the foundation with gold, silver, precious stones, wood, hay, straw—the work of each builder will become visible, for the Day will disclose it, because it will be revealed with fire, and the fire will test what sort of work each has done. If what has been built on the foundation survives, the builder will receive a reward. If the work is burned up, the builder will suffer loss; the builder will be saved, but only as through fire. Do you not know that you are God's temple and that God's Spirit dwells in you? If anyone destroys God's temple, God will destroy that person. For God's temple is holy, and you are that temple.

—1 Corinthians 3:10–17

Silence.

...God's temple is holy, and you are that temple...

144

Psalm 132:1–9 *Memento, Domine*

1 LORD, remember David, *
   and all the hardships he endured;

2 How he swore an oath to the LORD *
   and vowed a vow to the Mighty One of Jacob:

3 "I will not come under the roof of my house, *
   nor climb up into my bed;

4 I will not allow my eyes to sleep, *
   nor let my eyelids slumber;

5 Until I find a place for the LORD, *
   a dwelling for the Mighty One of Jacob."

6 "The ark! We heard it was in Ephratah; *
   we found it in the fields of Jearim.

7 Let us go to God's dwelling place; *
   let us fall upon our knees before his footstool."

8 Arise, O LORD, into your resting-place, *
   you and the ark of your strength.

9 Let your priests be clothed with righteousness; *
   let your faithful people sing with joy.

Prayer

You have called us into your service, Lord God,
   and given us a diversity of gifts
   with which to build upon foundations
         laid by countless others over the centuries;
make us so deeply mindful of the responsibility you have given us
   that we will build together a church that is your holy dwelling place;
through Jesus Christ our Lord. Amen.

IV. Christ's Gifts to the Church

A Reading from the Letter to the Ephesians

The gifts he gave were that some would be apostles, some prophets, some evangelists, some pastors and teachers, to equip the saints for the work of ministry, for building up the body of Christ, until all of us come to the unity of the faith and of the knowledge of the Son of God, to maturity, to the measure of the full stature of Christ. We must no longer be children, tossed to and fro and blown about by every wind of doctrine, by people's trickery, by their craftiness in deceitful scheming. But speaking the truth in love, we must grow up in every way into him who is the head, into Christ, from whom the whole body, joined and knit together by every ligament with which it is equipped, as each part is working properly, promotes the body's growth in building itself up in love.

—Ephesians 4:11–16

Silence.

...to equip the saints for the work of ministry...

Psalm 8 *Domine, Dominus noster*

1 O LORD our Governor, *
how exalted is your Name in all the world!

2 Out of the mouths of infants and children *
your majesty is praised above the heavens.

3 You have set up a stronghold against your adversaries, *
to quell the enemy and the avenger.

4 When I consider your heavens, the work of your fingers, *
the moon and the stars you have set in their courses,

5 What is man that you should be mindful of him? *
the son of man that you should seek him out?

6 You have made him but little lower than the angels; *
you adorn him with glory and honor;

7 You give him mastery over the works of your hands; *
you put all things under his feet:

8 All sheep and oxen, *
even the wild beasts of the field,

9 The birds of the air, the fish of the sea, *
   and whatsoever walks in the paths of the sea.

10 O LORD our Governor, *
    how exalted is your Name in all the world!

Prayer

Almighty God, you have built your Church
   upon the foundation of the apostles and prophets,
        Jesus Christ himself being the chief cornerstone:
Grant us so to be joined together in unity of spirit by their teaching,
   that we may be made a holy temple acceptable to you;
through Jesus Christ our Lord,
   who lives and reigns with you and the Holy Spirit,
   one God, for ever and ever. Amen.

—The Book of Common Prayer, p. 230

V. THE WORK OF MINISTRY

A Reading from the Second Letter to the Corinthians

Therefore, since it is by God's mercy that we are engaged in this ministry, we do not lose heart. We have renounced the shameful things that one hides; we refuse to practice cunning or to falsify God's word; but by the open statement of the truth we commend ourselves to the conscience of everyone in the sight of God. And even if our gospel is veiled, it is veiled to those who are perishing. In their case the god of this world has blinded the minds of the unbelievers, to keep them from seeing the light of the gospel of the glory of Christ, who is the image of God. For we do not proclaim ourselves; we proclaim Jesus Christ as Lord and ourselves as your slaves for Jesus' sake. For it is the God who said, "Let light shine out of darkness," who has shone in our hearts to give the light of the knowledge of the glory of God in the face of Jesus Christ. But we have this treasure in clay jars, so that it may be made clear that this extraordinary power belongs to God and does not come from us.

—2 Corinthians 4:1–7

Silence.

...ourselves your servants for Jesus' sake...

Psalm 101 *Misericordiam et judicium*

1 I will sing of mercy and justice; *
    to you, O LORD, will I sing praises.

2 I will strive to follow a blameless course;
    oh, when will you come to me? *
    I will walk with sincerity of heart within my house.

3 I will set no worthless thing before my eyes; *
    I hate the doers of evil deeds;
    they shall not remain with me.

4 A crooked heart shall be far from me; *
    I will not know evil.

5 Those who in secret slander their neighbors I will destroy; *
    those who have a haughty look and a proud
            heart I cannot abide.

6 My eyes are upon the faithful in the land, that they may
            dwell with me, *
    and only those who lead a blameless life shall
            be my servants.

7 Those who act deceitfully shall not dwell in my house, *
    and those who tell lies shall not continue in my sight.

8 I will soon destroy all the wicked in the land, *
    that I may root out all evildoers from the city of the LORD.

Prayer

Good and gracious Lord,
    your love is expressed in a constant outpouring of marvelous gifts,
    although we are unworthy vessels of your grace;
help us, we pray, so to receive and use your gifts
    that we may always reflect more faithfully
            the glory revealed to us in the face of your Son,
            our Lord and Savior, Jesus Christ. Amen.

VI. Mutual Ministry

A Reading from a Sermon of Augustine, Bishop of Hippo

Solicitude about my office as bishop has engrossed me since the time this burden was placed upon my shoulders, for I shall have to give a rigorous account. But what ought we to fear after receiving this grace of the episcopacy? We must fear the danger of being led astray by the honor it brings to us, instead of using that office for a fruitful ministry. Help me, therefore, by your prayers that he who has deigned to give me this charge may also deign to help me to bear my burden.

When you pray in this way for me, it is really for yourselves that you are praying. For what is the burden of which I am speaking but you? Pray that I may be strong, as I myself pray that you may not be burdensome. For, indeed, our Lord Jesus Christ would never have said that his burden was light if he did not bear it with the one who is charged with it. And you too, support me. In that way, according to the commandment of the Apostle, we shall bear one another's burdens, thus accomplishing the law of Christ. If he does not bear the burden with us, we succumb. If he does not carry us, we fall.

If what I am "for" you frightens me, what I am "with" you reassures me. For you, I am the bishop; with you, I am a Christian. "Bishop," this is the title of an office one has accepted to discharge; "Christian," that is the name of the grace one receives. Dangerous title! Salutary name! We are tossed around in the whirlpool of that activity as in an immense sea. But, reminding ourselves of the blood with which we were ransomed, and calmed by this thought, we enter, as it were, into a safe harbor.

The day I became a bishop, a burden was laid on my shoulders for which it will be no easy task to render an account. The honors I receive are for me an ever present cause of uneasiness. Indeed, it terrifies me to think that I could take more pleasure in the honor attached to my office, which is where its danger lies, than in your salvation, which ought to be its fruit. This is why being set above you fills me with alarm, whereas being with you gives me comfort. Danger lies in the first; salvation in the second.

And for you, "I also pray and warn you against failing to cooperate with the grace you receive from God." Make my ministry a fruitful one. You are God's garden, and you should therefore welcome the laborer who does the visible work of planting and watering the seed, even though the growth comes from one who works invisibly within you. Help me both by your prayers and by your obedience, for then it will be a pleasure for me, not to preside over you, but to serve you.

—Augustine, Readings for the Daily Office from the Early Church,
J. Robert Wright, ed., Church Publishing Incorporated, pp. 278–279

Silence.

...Help me by your prayers...

Psalm 100 *Jubilate Deo*

1 Be joyful in the LORD, all you lands; *
  serve the LORD with gladness
  and come before his presence with a song.

2 Know this: The LORD himself is God; *
  he himself has made us, and we are his;
  we are his people and the sheep of his pasture.

3 Enter his gates with thanksgiving;
  go into his courts with praise; *
  give thanks to him and call upon his Name.

4 For the LORD is good;
  his mercy is everlasting; *
  and his faithfulness endures from age to age.

Prayer

You have called each one of us, Lord God,
  to serve your people in the Church
  and to serve your people in the world,
and you have given us rich gifts for the fulfillment
  of the ministries you have given us;
pour out those gifts, we pray,
  on your Church in this place
  and especially on those who are called
          to the ministry of *bishop*
strengthen all of us to serve you in unity and faithfulness
  to the benefit of your people
          and the glory of your great Name. Amen.

CLOSING PRAYER

Thank you, good and gracious God,
    for this time of peace and prayer;
grant that the prayers we offer at this time
    may be effective toward the strengthening of your church;
grant that *N.* may be faithful in the ministry for which *he/she* has been chosen;
    that your word may speak through *his/her* lips;
    that your love may reach out through *his/her* hands;
    and that your will be done in the coming days,
    in *N.* and in all of us. Amen.

alternate readings

FOR THE SELECTION OR ORDINATION OF A PRIEST OR DEACON, OR CELEBRATION OF A NEW MINISTRY

A Reading from a Letter of Simon Patrick, Bishop of Ely, 1692

The blessed apostle St. Paul thought it so great an honor to be made a Christian, that he thought no words too lofty to express the dignity of their estate, which he calls not only our high calling, but our heavenly calling in Jesus Christ. I cannot think of this but it makes me reflect what an honor then it is to be made an (ordained) minister of Jesus Christ whose business it is to bring others into this glorious state of Christianity, and to breed them up in it and keep them in it.

What preferment is there comparable to this, to be constituted a servant and a minister of the King of Glory, a steward of the heavenly mysteries, and ambassador for Christ, a laborer in his vineyard or harvest; which implies indeed great pains, but carries in it also the great honor of sowing the seed of eternal life in human souls, and cultivating, that is preparing and making them fit to be carried into Christ's heavenly kingdom?

Think what an honor it is to serve the Lord Jesus, and what care he took of his flock; how invaluable the human souls are which he purchased with his blood: what an inestimable treasure the gospel of Christ is with which you are intrusted.

—Simon Patrick, Bishop of Ely, 1692

Silence.

...to serve the Lord Jesus...

FOR THE SELECTION OR INSTALLATION OF LAY MINISTERS

A Reading from the Book of Exodus

The next day Moses sat as judge for the people, while the people stood around him from morning until evening. When Moses' father-in-law saw all that he was doing for the people, he said, "What is this that you are doing for the people? Why do you sit alone, while all the people stand around you from morning until evening?" Moses said to his father-in-law, "Because the people come to me to inquire of God. When they have a dispute, they come to me and I decide between one person and another, and I make known to them the statutes and instructions of God." Moses' father-in-law said to him, "What you are doing is not good. You will surely wear yourself out, both you and these people with you. For the task is too heavy for you; you cannot do it alone. Now listen to me. I will give you counsel, and God be with you! You should represent the people before God, and you should bring their cases before God; teach them the statutes and instructions and make known to them the way they are to go and the things they are to do. You should also look for able men among all the people, men who fear God, are trustworthy, and hate dishonest gain; set such men over them as officers over thousands, hundreds, fifties, and tens. Let them sit as judges for the people at all times; let them bring every important case to you, but decide every minor case themselves. So it will be easier for you, and they will bear the burden with you. If you do this, and God so commands you, then you will be able to endure, and all these people will go to their home in peace." So Moses listened to his father-in-law and did all that he had said. Moses chose able men from all Israel and appointed them as heads over the people, as officers over thousands, hundreds, fifties, and tens. And they judged the people at all times; hard cases they brought to Moses, but any minor case they decided themselves.

—Exodus 18:13–26

...you cannot do it alone...